Sean Dooley is a Melbourne author who has worked as a
television comedy writer. He is a contributor to *The Age*,
ABC radio and 3RRR, writing and talking about birds,
environmental issues, sport and, well, anything, really.
But his greatest claim to fame is that in 2002 he broke the
Australian birdwatching record for seeing the most species
in the one year. He then wrote about it in *The Big Twitch*,
thereby publicly outing himself as a bird-nerd.

Sean Dooley

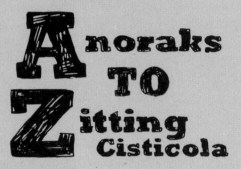

Anoraks TO Zitting Cisticola

a whole lot of stuff about BIRDWATCHING

Illustrations by MATT CLARE

ALLEN & UNWIN

First published in 2007

Allen & Unwin
83 Alexander Street
Crows Nest NSW 2065
Australia
Phone: (61 2) 8425 0100
Fax: (61 2) 9906 2218
Email: info@allenandunwin.com
Web: www.allenandunwin.com

National Library of Australia
Cataloguing-in-Publication entry:

Dooley, Sean, 1968- .
    Anoraks to Zitting Cisticola : a whole lot of stuff about birdwatching.
    1st ed.
    ISBN 9781741752724 (pbk.).
    1. Bird watching – Miscellanea. 2. Bird watching – Humor.
    3. Bird watchers – Miscellanea. 4. Bird watchers – Humor.
    I. Title.
598.07234

Author photo by Greg Elms
Edited by Sarah Brenan
Cover design by Matt Clare
Text design and layout by Pauline Haas
Printed in Australia by McPherson's Printing Group

10 9 8 7 6 5 4 3 2 1

To that lone, lost Glossy Ibis that turned up at Seaford Swamp when I was in Grade Six. Without the sheer thrill of seeing you from the schoolyard fence that lunchtime, none of this would ever have eventuated.

Welcome to birdwatching

The bayside suburb of St Kilda has long been seen as Melbourne's seedy underbelly, the equivalent of Sydney's King's Cross, London's Soho, or New York's Times Square. But as with most of those locations, a decade or two of gentrification has dimmed the red lights somewhat; these days, the only remaining street walkers left in St Kilda are likely to survive not so much because of the blind eye turned by the local vice squad, but due to the National Trust giving the hookers a heritage listing. So leaving my car in an off-street car park in St Kilda is no longer the anxiety-ridden exercise it may have once been.

I am surprised, therefore, to find a raucous gang busily partying on around my car. It is not a bunch of punks on the rampage but a flock of Musk Lorikeets feeding in the blossom of the flowering gums planted on the fringes of the car park. I stand transfixed, watching these dazzling green parrots screeching and squabbling as they stake out their claim over a particular cluster of nectar-rich blooms, seemingly oblivious to me and the other midday shoppers.

Just as oblivious are the shoppers who fail to notice these strident parrots and their carry-on. A pity really, as here in the middle of Australia's second-largest city is a flock of birds that, if seen in a zoo or on a wildlife special, would have those same shoppers cooing with appreciative wonder.

When people find out I am a birdwatcher, they often ask me where I go birdwatching, as if it is something that happens elsewhere, beyond the realm of everyday life. But while I enjoy nothing better than getting out into some remote wilderness to look for birds, the truth is that these car park lorikeets a mere five minutes from my home offer the quintessential birding experience.

Firstly, there is the sheer thrill of watching a wild bird go about its business; though I have seen thousands of Musk Lorikeets over the years, this close-up encounter jolts me back to the uncomplicated joy of watching birds that first got me into birding as a kid. But merely looking at a bird does not equate to birdwatching. If I were just bird-looking, the parrot I am looking at eye-to-eye would be a random pretty creature in a world of creatures, but because of my birdwatching I know it is a Musk Lorikeet. And furthermore, I know that it and its companions have come into this urban environment because the drought has dried up the supply of eucalypt nectar in the woodlands where they would normally reside at this time of year. By the process of identifying these Musk Lorikeets – giving a name to them – the encounter somehow becomes more meaningful, because I can now put the experience in some sort of context. To borrow the hideously reductive phrase of the economist, being a birdwatcher has *value added* to my viewing of these birds.

One might suspect that with all this awareness there is a danger I could become just a little bit smug; after all, nobody else in the car park is having the same insight into this parallel world happening in their midst. But any superiority I may be feeling is countered by an awareness of another sort, one that I often get while birding, particularly when it is somewhere so public. To the ordinary civilian, I look like an absolute dill standing there in a suburban car park gawping up into a tree.

Birdwatching can be an absolutely fantastic hobby. It brings many, many personal rewards. Freedom from public embarrassment, however, is certainly not one of them. I have been acutely aware of this since my first day at high school, when a sadist of a form teacher introduced me to a class of thirty adolescent boys I had never met before as a birdwatcher. While no longer ashamed of my passion, I have to admit that even I can see that there is something quite absurd about a grown man running around chasing after birds (of the feathered kind).

But sometimes my enthusiasm overrides my natural caution and I expose myself for the freak that I am, at heart. Recently, I was travelling on the ferry to Fraser Island in Queensland with a group of birders gathered for the annual Fraser Island Bird Week, I spied a couple of seabirds roosting on a navigational pylon. Knowing that members of the group had expressed an interest in seeing this particular species but forgetting that not all aboard the vessel were birdwatchers, I screamed to all and sundry: 'Boobies, Brown Boobies! I've got some boobies over here!'

The saddest thing is that not until much later did it even occur to me that what I had said could be possibly be misconstrued and that the odd looks I was getting were not because people were admiring me for remaining vigilant after a long day's birding, but because they were thinking, 'If this binocular-wearing pervert comes near my kids I'm calling security'.

Essentially this book is an attempt to explain why, since the age of ten, I have thrown myself into what those on the outside find an unfathomable obsession. I had been hoping to achieve this with the publication of *The Big Twitch* in 2005, my confessional of the year I spent travelling around Australia trying to break the record for seeing the most species of bird in the one year. I thought I had penned everything I would ever want to write about birds, birdwatchers and birdwatching and that I could move on with my life unburdened and finally understood. I imagined I would never again have to answer another question about my birdwatching addiction because I had, I believed, explained it all.

Within the first week of the book coming out I realised just how wrong I was. Rather than freeing me from my birding past, since publication I have been condemned to repeat it, spending more time explaining my obsession with birds than I had in the previous twenty years. I had outed myself as a birder and it turns out that there were a whole lot of bird-curious people closeted away who had all sorts of pent-up questions they wanted answered: What do you actually do? What are the mechanics of it? Do you need to wear a special costume? Does it hurt the first time you do it?

So this book is for all of you out there who have ever thought that birdwatching may be for you. I have tried to answer all your burning questions about birdwatching. Not the standard stuff like how to tell a Lemon-bellied Flycatcher from a Grey Whistler at fifty paces, but the useful gen that the field guides won't tell you: how to look cool in an anorak (answer: it's impossible); identification tips on recognising someone with Birdy-nerdy Syndrome and how to avoid being trapped at a party with them; how to fool a rarities committee; what is the correct birding etiquette for puking over the side of a boat while out seabirding; when is it appropriate to take a pish in polite company; right down to what the hell is a Zitting Cisticola, and is it contagious? You know, all the really important stuff.

But most of all, I've written this book for me. Hopefully with all your birding questions answered I can slink back to a life of birding obscurity and from now on whenever I am at a sewage farm watching birds, or at a restaurant having a meal, or packing my shopping into the back of the car in a St Kilda car park, and somebody comes up and asks me, 'Birdwatching hey? What's that all about?' I won't have to answer. I can just throw a copy of this book at them, and scream, 'Read this, it's all in there!'

The cheat's guide to using this book

In an ideal world, every reader would read this book from cover to cover. But in an ideal world I would have rock-hard abs, Collingwood would have won more than one flag in fifty years and I would have actually seen a Grey Falcon rather than drive thousands of kilometres to look at the branch other birders had seen one perching on.

So recognising the fact that most readers are likely to be dipping in and out of this book, according to either how long it takes for the bookseller to start looking suspiciously at you, or how long it is before another member of the family bangs on the toilet door asking how much longer you'll be, here is a quick way to get the most out of this book.

First, you need to determine your level of birdwatching experience. If you don't know your grasswren from your albatross then some entries may leave you totally mystified. Then again, if you are a gun twitcher (*see* GUN) with twenty years birding experience you are probably not going to read about what a chook is. I therefore recommend that all readers turn to the 'Q' section and try out the quiz. The results will place you into one of three categories: twitcher (hard-core, fanatical birder), birdwatcher (someone with a general interest in birds) or dude (a total novice).

For dudes

If you fell into the dude category, reading the following five entries will give you a good general introduction to both this book and the world of the birdwatcher:

Binoculars (page 21)
Birdy-nerdy Syndrome (page 32)
Field guides, how to use them (page 77)
Gonads (page 87)
List (page 129)

For birdwatchers

For those of you whom the quiz designated as birdwatchers, I'd suggest reading the following entries:

Binoculars, care (page 22)
Captain Twitchpants (page 40)
List of lists (page 132)
Nudity (page 152)
Uncle Trevor (page 237)

For twitchers

And if you are deemed to be a twitcher, your family has my deepest sympathy. You may, however, find these entries of particular interest:

Binoculars, as fashion accessories (page 24)
Fast-twitch muscles (page 67)
Hot spots (page 102)
Majizzmo (page 138)
Night Parrot (page 145)

From this entrée I am sure you will realise that there is a hell of a lot of stuff in the world of birdwatching, and hopefully with your appetite whetted, you will choose to throw yourself into the rest of this birding banquet. Happy feasting.

Anorak / an all-weather, waterproof coat, universally recognised as the uniform of the bird-nerd.

Seemingly more popular in the UK, the anorak doesn't often make an appearance here in Australia, due to it being exceptionally uncomfortable to wear in the heat. That and the fact that it hasn't rained across most of the country in the last ten years means that the anorak tends to stay in the back of a birder's wardrobe. Anoraks are most often seen on pelagic boat trips (*see* PELAGIC) where keeping dry and warm is a priority.

Looking cool in an anorak is *always* a big ask, as wearing one automatically makes you look like a trainspotter (*see* ASBIRDERS). Bill Oddie's aphorism that 'Seriousness is in inverse proportion to cleanliness' still rings true. You can't be taken seriously as a twitcher if your anorak isn't a little distressed, with at least one mysterious patch of grunge on the front. It may be fish oil from some shark liver berley, it may be some albatross shit acquired during a banding expedition, it may be a vomit stain from a previous boat trip – whatever its origin, that stain establishes your credentials as a hard-core birder (*see* PELAGIC).

Wearing anoraks that are bright yellow or fluoro orange is just not on (*see* CAMOUFLAGE), unless you want to say to the world that you are a seriously hard-core birder who goes out on seas so rough and dangerous in order to watch birds that there is every chance you may be swept overboard and need an outfit that can be spotted by search-and-rescue aircraft. This ploy doesn't work if you are in fact catching the ferry to Rottnest Island in order to tick off Common Pheasant and Peafowl; being introduced birds, these are hardly deemed risking your life for (*see* PLASTICS).

 ACTION: When acquiring an anorak, make sure to get one with lots of pockets. They come in handy for storing all sorts of things like notebooks, field guides and (most importantly) handfuls of food so that you don't have to go below deck on a pelagic trip where seasickness is almost guaranteed (*see* SEASICKNESS).

Asbirders Syndrome / a little-known offshoot of Asperger's Syndrome only recently discovered by researchers at the Big Twitch Institute. Also known as *Birdy-nerdy Syndrome*, it goes by the scientific name *Dorkus ornithologus*.

Asperger's Syndrome is a condition on the autism spectrum that severely hinders normal social development. People with Asperger's (usually men) are often good with hard facts and figures, but the emotional subtleties of everyday day life elude them They often become obsessed with a particular subject such as trains or dinosaurs or mechanical things, to the point where the only way they can interact with others is through the medium of their obsession which can leave them feeling quite isolated from the rest of society.

Throw in birds as the object of fascination, and you've got yourself a classic case of Asbirders . . .

Typical Asbirders sufferers are usually male, socially inadequate and obsessed with watching birds to the exclusion of everything else, particularly relationships and social niceties. Often they become so fixated on birds that it is like obsessive-compulsive disorder without the compulsive bit (unless you consider that checking the Internet every fifteen minutes to see if a rare bird has turned up is compulsive). In a social situation when you are talking about your job or relationship problems or the fact that you have only five minutes to live, the Asbirder will always turn the conversation back to birds.

When I wrote about Asperger's in *The Big Twitch* (the term Asbirder had yet to be invented) I was quite torn. Here I was, admittedly in light-hearted fashion, accusing a group of people I considered dear friends of suffering from a serious disorder. I was expecting retribution but it never came. Then it hit me. Sure, birders had all gone out and bought my book, but that didn't mean they actually bothered to read it. Ignoring all that boring story crap, they had turned straight to the list at the end to see where I saw Carpentarian Grasswren, or whether I managed to get Papuan Flowerpecker in the Torres Strait.

So, if you're still not sure whether or not you are an Asbirders sufferer, why not take the following quick quiz, opposite, for a bit of self-diagnosis?

 ACTION: If you are trapped in a conversation with an Asbirder, simply start talking about your feelings. That should shut them up instantly.

DIY IDENTIFICATION **ASBIRDERS SYNDROME QUIZ**

1 Does it bother you that Anorak and Asbirders appear before Albatross in this chapter, even though they don't come before albatross alphabetically?

A: Yes.

B: No.

C: I am skipping this quiz and going to the bit about albatrosses.

2 Which causes you more confusion: the wing structure of golden plovers, or working out when your partner is in a bad mood?

A: Wing structure of golden plovers.

B: Mood of partner.

C: I have never had a partner.

3 Your partner (just pretend you have one if you answered (c) to the last question) takes you on a romantic balloon ride, pulls out an engagement ring, looks you in the eye, and asks you to marry them. What is your first thought?

A: I want to spend the rest of my life with this gorgeous person.

B: Their eyes are such a beautiful blue … like on the undertail coverts of a Bourke's Parrot.

C: I bet I could get some brilliant flight shots of White-throated Needletails from up here.

4 When was the last time you had a lengthy conversation that wasn't primarily about birds?

A: Last week.

B: Last month.

C: I've never had a proper conversation.

5 Somebody is looking at you with their brow furrowed and the corner of their mouth turned down as you talk to them. What does the way they look make you think?

A: They are unhappy with you because you have spent the last twenty minutes talking about the nesting Brown Goshawks you have been monitoring.

B: They are unhappy with you because they too would like to see the Brown Goshawks at the nest.

C: They look like a Brown Goshawk.

Give yourself 10 points for every time you answered (c), 5 points for every (b) and no points for (a).

YOUR SCORE:

25–50 points: You definitely have Asbirders. But don't worry, though you may be socially isolated, you probably have a good job in some field like engineering or computer programming. So sit back and enjoy the birds. This is your century.

10–25 points: You most definitely have strong Asbirders tendencies. Chances are you are just aware enough to realise that you have them and feel guilty about your actions, but not quite aware enough to alter your patterns of behaviour.

0–10 points: Let's face it, you probably have Asbirders as well. Why else would you bother with such an obviously bogus quiz?

Albatross / **1.** ocean-going birds noted for their long wings and graceful flight. **2.** a score in golf three below par. Anyone claiming one would be, in birding terms, labelled a stringer (*see* STRINGER).

With a massive wingspan that allows it to ply the ocean waves for months at a time, the graceful albatross has long inspired poets (*see* RIME OF THE ANCIENT MARINER), but in a case of life imitating art, we, like the mariner, are killing our albatrosses as we bring natural disaster upon ourselves. Nine species of albatross regularly visit Australian waters (or thirteen or twenty depending on which species concept you subscribe to – *see* SPECIES), almost all of which are in imminent threat of extinction from long-line fishing.

Long-line fishing involves baiting lines up to several kilometres long behind an ocean-going trawler. The albatross are attracted by the baited hooks floating on the surface. They latch onto the bait, get caught by the hooks and are dragged under and drowned when the line eventually sinks. In some albatross populations, this has reduced numbers by up to 85 per cent in less than twenty years.

This should be one of the easiest conservation problems to solve by means of simple measures such as setting the lines at night, putting weights on the line, or even unfreezing the bait before it is set so that it sinks more quickly. However, the legal fishing industry has been slow to address the issue and, with so many illegal boats out there, it is going to be an incredibly hard job to reverse the trend.

 ACTION: There is a concerted campaign led by Birdlife International to help try and save the albatross. Further details can be found on the websites:
www.birdlife.org/action/campaigns/save_the_albatross
www.savethealbatross.net

Armchair ticks / not an affliction, and not birds literally seen from an armchair, but birds that are added to a birder's list after the event due to taxonomic or other changes (*see* CHECKLIST, TICK).

There are people who really do birdwatch from a chair, both real birds (called a 'Big Sit') and the birds they see on television (called 'Man, you really need to get a life'). But usually an armchair tick happens when a former subspecies is split and given full species status. Sometimes it can happen in other ways, as when that unidentified snipe you saw at Broome is later caught and definitively identified as a Swinhoe's Snipe. Never quite as satisfying as identifying a bird at the time you see it, an armchair tick is still a tick nonetheless.

Atlas / *The Atlas of Australian Birds* is an ongoing bird-mapping project run by Birds Australia.

The first Atlas began as a one-off project between the years 1977 and 1981. Thousands of birdwatchers around Australia reported their sightings to a central database, forming a snapshot of where our birds were during this period. A follow-up project with over 7000 volunteers was begun in 1998, primarily to track the changes to our avifauna (*see* AVIFAUNA) over that time.

Even more comprehensive than the original, the new Atlas, published in 2003, painted a generally depressing picture. While some birds had increased in range and numbers, a sizeable number of our bird species, particularly our woodland and grassland birds, had suffered a decline. Here was direct evidence that the clearing of woodlands and grasslands was having an effect on our wildlife.

Birds Australia is still running the Atlas project, and I urge every birder to get involved. Birding is one of the few hobbies that allows you to contribute directly to the body of scientific knowledge – but not if all those records stay locked in your head, or on the notebooks on your shelf. You're probably thinking you'll get around to sorting through all your records 'one day'. Let's face it, it's never going to happen, and when you die, your family are going to hire a big skip to throw all your notebooks into, along with all your newspapers, fast-food table napkins and Bachman-Turner Overdrive albums.

But be warned, if you are going to submit records of your sightings to the Atlas, they will (shock horror) be subjected to a vetting process. For some birders, even the mere thought that they could be put under any sort of scrutiny is a mortal wound to their proud reputation. Some birders simply do not like to be questioned, despite the verification process being for the sake of scientific accuracy. They refuse to countenance that they could ever make a mistake, even if it was merely a transcription error on the Atlas form.

These are the types who thunder against what they see as self-appointed snooty experts such as Birds Australia as being examples of the 'Birding Police' whose mission seems to be to bring down the enjoyment of the innocent birdwatcher just trying to enjoy their hobby. It makes me wonder what else the Birding Police must get up to. Are they the ones pulling cars over on lonely country roads and asking, 'Excuse me driver, how many birds have you seen this evening?' Or perhaps they are the ones monitoring safe birdwatching facilities or setting up controversial new heron trials to help deal with the epidemic of birdwatching addiction sweeping the country.

ACTION: If you are prepared to run the gauntlet of the Birding Police and would like to join the Atlas scheme, the best point of contact would be: atlas@birdsaustralia.com.au or check out the Atlas website at www.birdata.com.au

Australia / a country south of New Guinea, west of New Zealand and a long way east of Africa. Australia has 5 per cent of the world's land mass but around 8 per cent of the world's bird species.

In the past 220 years, around 840 species of bird have been recorded in Australia, although if you took its external territories out of the mix that number would drop under the 800 mark. So in terms of diversity, it has half as many species as Colombia and more than twice as many as New Zealand (*see* SPECIES, TAXONOMY, EXTERNAL TERRITORIES).

Not that it would be easy to see all 840 species. No birder has yet managed to crack 800 species in their lifetime, though Australia's champion twitcher is currently only nine shy of that milestone.

This is because around 600 species breed here in any given year, while another 130-odd are non-breeding migrants or visitors. This leaves another 100 or so that are considered vagrant occurrences, birds from elsewhere that have turned up here accidentally (*see* VAGRANT), such as the Upland Sandpiper, which has only been seen here once in 1848, or the Grey Heron which, if you missed the first Australian record in 1839, you would have had to wait until 2002 to see it again!

Based on membership figures for birding organisations, out of a population of 20 million, Australia has around 10 000 people who would call themselves birdwatchers. This is a whopping 0.05 per cent of the Australian population, though as some of the major bird books have sold over 40 000 copies, there are probably a lot more people out there with at least a passing interest in birds.

By way of comparison, membership of the RSPB, Britain's peak birding organisation is around 1.1 million, or about 1.8 per cent of the population. In Australia this would equate to 360 000 birders roaming our swamps, forests and sewage farms, which would be a great boon for the cause of conservation and eco-tourism, but those curmudgeonly birders (like myself) who like to go birdwatching for the birds, not the birdwatchers, would have to switch to even more obscure pastimes such as snail wrangling, collecting toenail clippings or voting for the Democrats.

Australian Capital Territory / with Canberra at its centre, the ACT is home to both our national government and video porn industry, both of which allow Australians to watch other people rooting things.

The ACT is often overlooked as a stopover on the birding trail, but that doesn't mean there aren't some good birds to be had; around 280 species have been seen, including highlights such as Superb Lyrebird, Speckled Warbler, Glossy Black and Gang-gang Cockatoo and Spotted Quail-thrush.

The best birding sites include Jerrabomberra Wetlands, Campbell Park, Tidbinbilla Nature Reserve and Mulligan's Flat Nature Park. Between them, they cover a range of habitats from wet forest to grassy woodlands and wetlands.

There are probably more birders per head of population in the ACT than in any other Australian state or territory. This is not that surprising when you consider how many academics and public servants work and live there; there's no getting around it, eggheads really get off on hobbies like birdwatching. The main local birding group is the Canberra Ornithologists' Group (see, even the name sounds boffinish) and they are well organised with regular meetings, outings and special projects such as the Garden Bird Survey which has been going continuously since 1981.

 ACTION: Canberra Ornithologists' group can be contacted at: http://canberrabirds.org.au, or write to:
The Secretary, COG
PO Box 301
Civic Square,
ACT 2608

Autumn / the season of the year marking the transition between summer and winter; in Australia, usually considered to cover the months of March, April and May, though in the northern half of the continent it doesn't really exist because at some time in late March or early April the climate suddenly goes from hot and wet one day to hot and dry the next.

In the south, by the beginning of March most spring and summer breeders have raised their young, and are pretty quiet, though if it has been a good wet season up north, or there have been big thunderstorms in the outback, the breeding season may be in full swing. This can be the best time to visit the Centre, as there is a flush of activity and the temperatures, while still capable of reaching 40 degrees, are generally far more bearable than the unrelenting, searing summer heat.

Autumn is when the migrants head off. The waders gather in massive flocks for a last pre-flight feast in departure-lounge areas such as Broome and the Gulf of Carpentaria (*see* WADER). Many bush birds slip off to their wintering grounds in north Queensland, New Guinea and beyond. Others, such as Yellow-faced and other honeyeaters, put on quite a show as they make their way up the east coast, sometimes in very large numbers. Winter migrants start to make their move: Flame Robins come down from the mountains and Double-banded Plovers arrive from New Zealand, while Orange-bellied and Swift Parrots, along with some other Tassie birds, make the treacherous Bass Strait crossing.

As the nights grow shorter and the days cooler, the weather patterns for much of the country are far more settled and it feels as if the bird population is taking a deep breath before the onset of winter. It feels like a time of calm reflection – certainly not as many vagrants turn up as in spring or summer, so there is less action for the twitcher (*see* VAGRANT).

Knowing they can't compete with twitching, most of the major football codes choose to start their season in autumn, waiting for the lull to try and lure fans away from the higher profiled sport. But come the first big albatross-laden Southerly Buster, the football authorities are resigned to the fact that their weekly attendances will drop from something like half a million a weekend to 499 992. And they know they are helpless to do anything about it.

Avifauna / a fancy word for birds, specifically when talking about birds in large numbers or across many species; a legitimate scientific term, though most often used by try-hard writers to convince people that they have, at least, an ounce of scientific credibility (*see* ATLAS).

Bifcus / a contraction used by some birders for Black-faced Cuckoo-shrike.

As if giving birds ridiculous sounding names isn't bad enough, birders have a habit of making their nicknames just as ludicrous. 'Bifcus' is one of the most widely used of these. Occasionally the White-bellied Cuckoo-shrike is referred to as 'Wibcus', though thankfully, I have never heard anyone refer to the Moluccan Cuckoo-shrike as 'Mucus'.

Big Day / the one-day cricket of the birding world; a 24-hour birdwatching event, where participants try to see or hear as many birds as possible in a calendar day (midnight to midnight).

In Australia, The Big Day has been somewhat overshadowed by the Twitchathon (*see* TWITCHATHON), a 24-hour contest which usually runs over the course of two days (i.e. 4 p.m. Saturday to 4 p.m. Sunday). My personal Big Day record is 195 species, which pales into insignificance when compared with the almost unbelievable Australian record of 247 birds seen by a group of north Queensland birders in 1998! So unbelievable, in fact, that some birders have called for their race-day swabs to be tested for traces of string (*see* STRINGERS).

The Big Twitch / the totally spurious and unreliable memoir of a clearly delusional twitcher recounting his fantasy of seeing 703-plus species in 2002 to break the Australian Big Year record.

 ACTION: This book is so audaciously bogus that if you haven't already got a copy I suggest you go out and buy one, if only to see what this crank believes he can get away with. Better still, buy a second copy and share the incredulity around.

The Big Twitch Institute / the highly esteemed and not-at-all made up research institute that supplies much of the raw data for this book.

Bold, sometimes controversial, but always 104 per cent scientifically accurate, The Big Twitch Institute tackles the really big issues in birdwatching that no one else is prepared to take on – topics such as how to look cool whilst wearing binoculars, how long is a piece of string and why male birdwatchers don't have girlfriends (*see* BINOCULARS AS FASHION ACCESSORIES, STRINGER, GIRLFRIENDS).

Big Year / applying the principles of a Big Day for 365 days of the year; a birding marathon where the aim is to build the biggest year list.

The Australian Big Year record of 703 species was set in 2002. At the time of writing (2007), nobody had been stupid enough to give up a year of their time and a substantial chunk of their savings, not to mention their sanity, to try and break it. For this I am truly grateful because to try to claim the record back would, I am sure, come close to killing me!

Binoculars / an optical device used by both eyes at once designed to magnify a distant image; field glasses. Also known as bins, binos, (rhymes with winos), or binox if you must, but please never noccies, unless you are at least a grandparent or using the term in an ironic way.

Though you can still go birding without a pair of binoculars around your neck, they do make life a hell of a lot easier for both you and the birds. In essence, binoculars bring the birds closer to you without you having to get too close to them.

If you can't afford to fork out the two or three thousand dollars required for top-notch binoculars, you will still be able to pick up a perfectly serviceable pair for under a couple of hundred. Just try not to look through other birders' snazzy pair of bins as it will just depress you. When viewed through a really good pair of you-beaut bins even boring birds like sparrows seem as vibrant as a bird of paradise. It will make you never want to go back to your old pair, especially if they are one of the shoddily made cheapies where it would be more effective to just rub sand into your eyes.

Even more perplexing to the beginner than the plethora of binocular brands and models is the numbers printed on nearly every pair (8x30, 10x50, 7x42). These merely describe the magnification power and field of view of the binoculars. The first number is the magnification – the higher the number, the greater the magnification. The second number refers to the diameter in millimetres of the objective lens (the lens at the opposite end to where your eye goes). A higher second number means that the lens is wider and therefore lets in more light.

On this basis you would assume that the a pair of 30x100 bins would be much better for obtaining close-up views than a pair of 8x25s. Perhaps, but the binoculars would be so big and heavy you would develop Popeye arms just holding them, and a Popeye squint from trying to focus, as anything above a 10 magnification becomes too difficult to keep the image still.

My preferred option is 10x42. For many twitchers, these are still too heavy and powerful and they would opt for an 8x30, but I must say I like something a bit more substantial to hold onto. Anything below a 7 magnification is useless, in my opinion; you may as well just use your naked eyes. Those who favour the 8 say correctly that you can use them up extremely close without losing focus, and this is handy for situations where you are birding in dense bush. Again I say, if you are that close to the bird, why not use your eyes?

Binoculars, care / what your most important piece of birding equipment deserves.

I have to confess: I treat my binoculars rather shabbily. One birder that borrowed them likened the state of the lenses to the bottom of a budgie cage. I am therefore not a good role model when it comes to care of binoculars, but the following tips do work.

You should actually not try to clean the lenses too often, as you risk rubbing off the polished surfaces and tinting that enhance the light-gathering capabilities of your bins. When you do clean them, a fine brush for removing dust and particles and a soft cloth for cleaning the surface are best. Often you get these with the bins themselves. Avoid tissues, as they are often impregnated with fragrant oils which may affect the lens coatings.

The best way of keeping your binoculars clean is to put them away when you are eating. This may go against your desire to be constantly loud and proud that you are a birder, but it will mean that you don't drop food on them accidentally. I knew one birder who was inconsolable when he accidentally dropped a bit of chocolate onto his brand new bins. Even years down the track, the mention of this incident could still bring a tear to his eye, and his voice would crack as he tried to explain: 'You don't understand, chocolate stains can be really hard to remove.'

Putting your binoculars in their case avoids this situation but is more likely to lead to the next scenario, which is accidentally leaving the binoculars on the roof of the car. Often the bins are heavy enough to remain on the roof for the journey, but the story ends in disaster when the birder suddenly realises what's happened and screams out to the driver, 'Stop the car!' The driver slams on the brakes and the bins sail forward, crashing onto the road ahead.

This is when the real damage is done, even if the lenses don't smash, because the prisms are likely to go out of alignment due to the impact. When one prism goes out of alignment with the one in the other barrel, you end up cross-eyed trying to focus them.

The prisms in my first-ever pair of binoculars fell out of alignment after the strap broke. (There's another tip: the strap will usually be the first part of the bins to wear out, so to avoid future grief, you may as well replace it with a reliable one as soon as you purchase your new set.) They were fairly primitive binoculars and I simply opened them up, took the prisms out and literally dropped them back in. Amazingly, it worked and they realigned perfectly. Later I had misaligned prisms in another pair, and because I knew that to open the casing would cause irreparable damage to the binoculars, I spent years squinting through them with one eye. If the prisms fall out of alignment in modern binoculars, the best thing you can do is admit defeat and get them fixed by a professional.

One final useful tip: most binoculars these days are allegedly waterproof. If you are positive yours are, make sure you carry a small bottle of fresh water with you when on a boat trip or anywhere you are getting salt spray on the lenses. Rather than constantly trying to rub the lenses clean (which is only going to grind salt into them), simply pour a little of the water over them. It will soon dry and you will get a clear view again, at least until the next wave comes crashing over the top of the boat, which on the pelagic trips off southern Australia in winter is usually about eight seconds later (*see* PELAGIC).

Binoculars, as fashion accessories / an oxymoron. As essential as binoculars are, nobody has yet come up with a design that enables the user to look cool while wearing them.

Think of the coolest person you can – James Dean, David Bowie, Dannii Minogue (I'm sure someone thinks she is cool). Now imagine them with a pair of binoculars around their neck. See? Even they couldn't pull it off, so how could your average dorky birdwatcher?

Exacerbating the problem is that most good birders have their binoculars sitting as high on the chest as possible. They do it for very practical reasons – so they can whip the binoculars up to the eyes in a split second to grab that identity-nailing view – but God, it looks nerdy.

For years I resisted and kept my binocular strap as low-slung as possible, like Clint Eastwood's holster or Keith Richards's Fender Telecaster. As sexy as it could get with binoculars, thought I. But not only was I slow in getting my bins up to my eyes, I also found, when I was running after a departing bird, that they had a tendency to come crashing down hard onto my goolies, leaving me doubled over in pain in the middle of a field while everyone else was copping magnificent views of that Orange-bellied Parrot.

 ACTION: Even though it is incredibly daggy and liable to attract the ire of anti-greenie types, it is very important to wear your binoculars at all times when out birding, particularly in rural areas, even when going into town. If locals see enough birders in their district – especially when they are spending money in the towns – it may eventually click that, without the birds, you and your money wouldn't be there. It may just help them to reassess the value of conserving habitat. Well, that's what I hope for, and why I put up with all the 'poofter' jibes.

Binoculars, how to use them / coordinating hands, eyes and brain in an attempt to focus on something that is very small, a long way away, and constantly moving about.

Those who have been birdwatching for years often forget how very frustrating it can be for novices to get the hang of using binoculars; it can literally leave you with a headache. But this is one area where practice and persistence does make things a lot easier. To get you started, here are a few tips.

1. Practise focusing on non-moving objects like trees, fence posts or billboards, to get the hang of how your bins work.

2. Try to find the bird with your eyes before you look through the binoculars at it. Even the best bins have a highly limited field of vision compared to your eyes. When targeting a specific bird, you will waste too much precious time if you are spraying your binoculars around like a searchlight in a bombing raid.

3. For those with glasses, many modern binoculars have soft eyepieces that you can pop in or out so that the lens is flush against your specs – you don't need to take them off every time you want to look at a bird.

4. When looking for a bird in the canopy, rather than searching blindly through the leaves, start at the base of the tree you know the bird is in and work your way upwards so that you have a sense of where you are.

5. If you are initially having trouble focusing with both eyes, just close an eye and use the lens as a monocular until you have actually found the bird. It is better to see it with one eye than with blurred cross-eyes.

6. It is not advisable to use your binoculars to check out your birding companion if you fancy them. Even birdwatchers find this a bit creepy. If you must do it, be subtle.

Bird / the type of creature that inspires all this twitching madness; at heart the reason why every birder, be they twitcher, scientist, duffer, dude or buntie initially gets into this hobby (*see* TWITCHER, DUFFER, DUDE, BUNTIE).

Birds are incredible creatures. They fly while we are earthbound; they appear in a dazzling array of colours and forms; they sing in a multitude of voices. And they are pretty much everywhere. From the icy wastelands of the Antarctic continent to the air above Mount Everest and everywhere in between, it is possible to find birds.

Sometimes being a birdwatcher takes you into an arcane world of politics, personalities, lists and scientific debate, but every so often there will be an encounter with a bird – the way the light reflects off the plumage of Shining Bronze-Cuckoo in the morning sun, a Wedge-tailed Eagle soaring in a thermal, sitting eye to eye on the rainforest floor with a Tooth-billed Bowerbird – that absolutely delights and enchants and uplifts your spirits.

Birds – I can highly recommend them.

Bird bander / somebody who catches a bird, puts a band around its leg so that it can be identified in future scientific studies, and then lets it go (gee, bird people know how to have fun, don't they?); in Britain, known as ringers.

In Australia, bird banders have to undergo training before they are qualified to band birds and all banding projects have to obtain approval on their scientific and ethical merits. Even so, some people object to banding, claiming that capturing wild birds for any purpose is too stressful for the birds. Yet much of what we know about our birds has arisen through banding projects, and without knowledge of a creature it is very hard to protect it. So I am generally in favour of banding, as the long-term scientific gains it provides outweigh the short-term distress it may cause for individual birds.

I was involved in banding very early on in my birding career. On a personal level, it was extremely informative and inspirational to have such close-up contact with birds. I don't do go banding now, not due to ethical considerations, but because when you are banding you are tied to the one spot; checking the nets and processing any birds that are caught, or waiting for hours in the vain hope that something will be stupid enough to fly into the net. This is valuable time that I could be tearing up and down the countryside looking for birds. What can I say? I'm shallow and there is not much reward for the rabid twitcher in bird banding, though occasionally the bander has the last laugh, such as the wader banders who caught Australia's first Short-billed Dowitcher (*see* DOWITCHER, WADER BANDER) or the bloke in Thailand who recently rediscovered the Large-billed Reed-warbler after it had been presumed extinct for a century or so.

 ACTION: Details of the Australian Bird and Bat Banding Scheme (ABBBS) can be found at: www.environment.gov.au/biodiversity/science/abbbs

Birder / a contraction of the word birdwatcher; the term birdwatchers call themselves in the vain hope of seeming cool.

Even though they hate it, members of motorcycle gangs (a seriously tough group of dudes) are often called bikies rather than bikers by outsiders. So it seems rather hilarious that birders are never labelled birdies. Clearly a bunch of chain-wielding, leather jacket-wearing Hells Angels must be far less intimidating than a gaggle of binocular holding, anorak-clad bird-nerds.

A bird in the hand / for birdwatchers this colloquial saying is total rubbish, as a bird in the hand does not count as a tick unless it is your hand that it is in (*see* RULES OF TWITCHING).

Once somebody has a bird in the hand, it is technically no longer free-flying so it shouldn't be counted on your list. This would mean that if you were out with a bird bander and an Oriental Reed-Warbler flew into his mist net, if you saw it before the bander extracted it from the net, the reed-warbler would count for your list. If the bander got there first then technically it would not be a tick for you. This would be such an unbearable grip-off (*see* GRIPPING OFF) that I would seriously be tempted to tick the bloody thing anyway (*see* TICK).

But what happens if you see the bird after it has been released from the hand? Is it tickable then?

Recently, a Westland Petrel, a New Zealand seabird rarely seen in Australian waters, blew ashore on the New South Wales Central Coast. It was nursed back to health by a wildlife carer (*see* INJURED BIRDS) and set free on a pelagic boat trip (*see* PELAGIC) several months later. As the bird was released, the question arose from those on board who had never previously seen a Westland Petrel as to whether they could add it to their lists. The harsh answer was no – it was not as if the bird had arrived in their field of vision under its own steam.

That gave rise to another question: what if the bird flew off, disappeared over the horizon, then turned around and flew back past them again? Could they tick it then? The Westland would now be a free-flying bird, operating under its own steam. Sure, the origin of its journey was artificially imposed but it would now be in its natural environment doing what it normally did, in the same general area it had been doing it in before it got blown off course.

Some purists would say that they could definitely not tick it. But these are the types who would go so far as to refuse to tick off a bird if it has been banded, because the bird has been sullied by human hands and, therefore, somehow not legitimately 'wild'. They may be technically correct but, like all fundamentalists, they are absolutely no fun to be around.

Bird-nerd / once the favoured taunt of school-yard bullies towards kids who were into bird-watching.

However, in this era of Bill Gates and his cohort of billionaire computer geeks, nerd is the new cool and birdwatchers everywhere are scrambling to fess up to being bird-nerds. Of course the fickle wheel of cultural fashion will turn once more and, when it does, the bird-nerd will be left exposed, friendless and with their underpants wedged up past their binocular strap.

Birding-aus / an Internet list server about Australian birding matters.

A fabulous and increasingly indispensable reference point for the modern birder, and home to some of the kookiest nutters on the web (*see* INTERNET), where you can find out about the latest rare bird sighting, or join in a totally impassioned debate over the correct term to describe the leg colour of a Yellow-throated Scrubwren.

 ACTION: Go to the Birding-aus home address: www. shc.melb.catholic.edu.au/home/birding or you can try birdingonthe.net/mailinglists/AUSB.html if you want to quickly check out what has been posted to Birding-aus in the previous few days.

Birdo / an Australian alternative to 'birder', because we just love to whack an 'o' or a 'y' onto the end of words.

Birdo won out over birdy because, well, birdy just sounds naff. Use of the term seems to be dying out somewhat, along with other Australian vernacular such as 'bonza', 'dinkum' and 'a fair go for all'.

Birds Australia (BA) / the largest birding organisation in Australia, founded in 1901 as the Royal Australasian Ornithologists' Union.

In the 1990s, this mouthful of a name changed to the more manageable Birds Australia, reflecting the shift from a body solely concerned with the scientific study of birds, to a broader organisation encompassing research and conservation. They even have social activities these days.

For an organisation that receives little funding, doesn't have a massive membership base and still relies heavily on the goodwill of volunteers, Birds Australia gets a lot done. In the past few years it has produced the final volumes of *The Handbook of Australian, New Zealand and Antarctic Birds* (*see HANZAB*); continued the second Atlas project; run multiple ongoing bird conservation projects; managed observatories and conservation reserves; published scientific journals and members magazines; hosted annual scientific congresses; worked with rural landholders; lobbied governments on bird conservation and welfare issues; and, best of all, employed a swag of bird-nerds, some of the most unemployable members on the planet – they even managed to get me a job once.

ACTION: To join Birds Australia, either go to its website, www.birdsaustralia.com.au, or drop a line to:

Birds Australia:
The Green Building
60 Leicester Street
Carlton, Victoria
Australia, 3053

Birdy-nerdy Syndrome / another name for Asbirders Syndrome (*see* ASBIRDERS SYNDROME).

Physical signs of the syndrome sufferer include: well-developed neck muscles (from looking into tall trees at birds); a natural inclination towards anoraks; and the ability to talk under wet cement about the differences between juvenile and immature plumage in flycatchers.

Blockers / an English twitching term that is only just starting to gain currency here, describing a bird that turns up so infrequently that many years may elapse between sightings. Thus, the people who haven't seen the bird are blocked in their ability to catch up with the lists of those who have.

A classic blocker in the Australian sense would be the Red-legged Crake, which first appeared in Australia in Broome in 1958. It was not seen in Australia again until a presumably cyclone-driven bird appeared at a mining camp in Western Australia's Pilbara region in 2007. As I was unable to go for this bird, those who did now have a blocker over me, and only in the unlikely event that another turns up will I ever get a chance to 'unblock' the Red-legged Crake.

For the twitcher, a blocker is more desperately sought after than any other type of new bird for the list – the stakes are so much higher. If a twitcher misses out on a Grey Grasswren, it is no huge deal; although rare and hard to see, they are confined to the one area and won't go wandering too far, so all that is required of the twitcher is another visit to the Grey Grasswren's home turf.

By comparison, the Red-legged Crake is playing an away fixture. It may turn up again or it may not – you just never know. It is as if you were a Stones fan and missed out on their 1973 concert. Though upset at the time, you might reasonably presume they would come back to play again. If you had still not seen them by 2007, you might be rather more worried about ever seeing them play live, particularly every time Keith falls out of another coconut tree.

BOCA (formerly the Bird Observers' Club of Australia) / one of only two nation-wide organisations for birdwatchers.

Founded in 1905, BOCA (Bird Observation and Conservation Australia) has traditionally been more focused on the social side of birdwatching than its Birds Australia counterpart. BOCA has recently taken up more of a conservation focus (hence the name change), but still maintains its core program of outings to enable birders to share their hobby with others. There are 20 regional BOCA branches that operate semi-autonomously, often running their own meetings and trips.

In the past, the general difference between the two national organisations could be described loosely as BOCA being a club for those who liked to watch birds and BA being for those who liked to study birds. Or to put it another way, people thought of BA as full of serious eggheads, whereas

BOCA people liked to have a little fun while they went birding. Like all generalisations, these are far from the mark. As a sixteen-year-old, when I ended up at a BOCA camp on New Year's Eve, I would have heartily disagreed with anyone who said BOCA people had fun. I wasn't fazed by the fact that there were only three people aside from me under 40, but was blown away when all of them went to bed by nine o'clock!

 ACTION: To join BOCA, either go to their website, www.birdobservers.org.au
or contact them at their Melbourne office:
> BOCA
> PO Box 185
> Nunawading, Victoria,
> Australia 3131
> Tel: 03 9877 5342

Bore / 1. a deep hole of small diameter drilled into the aquifer of an artesian basin through which water rises under hydrostatic pressure. **2.** a birdwatcher whose unilateral ramblings about birds makes you want to drill a hole through your skull into your brain to relieve the pressure of such an interminably dull monologue.

Artesian bores are actually surprisingly good places to look for birds. They may look like environmental disaster zones thanks to the cattle that dutifully make their way to drink at them every day, chewing every blade of edible greenery to the nub and trampling everything else to dust under their hard, introduced hooves. But because a bore is often the only water in a desert landscape, it is amazing just how many different birds will congregate there, especially seed-eaters such as parrots and pigeons that don't get much moisture from their food. Setting yourself up by a bore at dawn or dusk is a particularly good way of seeing the elusive Flock Bronzewing.

Remember that most bores are located on private property, so it is best not to camp right beside them; the landowners can get justifiably shirty if they think their cattle and sheep have been scared off by your presence. Even more advisable is to avoid conducting your ablutions in the bore's water, no matter how tempting. I heard of one landowner who happened upon a family waist-deep in a bore's dam, the only source of fresh water on the property, lathered to the hilt in soap.

Some landowners are great value and very birder-friendly. Others want nothing better than to find a reason to ban visitors from their properties, so a little commonsense and the occasional touch of selflessness would be of benefit to all who visit after you.

Buff-breasted Button-quail / one of the least-known of Australia's endemic birds, the Buff-breasted Button-quail has never been photographed or had its call recorded in the wild.

The habits of the Buff-breasted Button-quail are not well known and sightings in its known range, which centres on the tropical woodlands with a grassy understorey of Cape York Peninsula, are very infrequent.

But here's a red-hot tip for you: if you want to see this species, wait until I am writing a book. This bird has only been twitchable twice this century, both times while I was deskbound, frantically rushing to meet my publisher's deadline and therefore unable to go twitch them. It remains one of a handful of Australian breeding species that I have not seen. So if you were to commission me to write a third book, I can absolutely guarantee that a Buff-breasted Button-quail will turn up, which you can happily twitch while I am stuck at my desk.

Buntie / a certain type of lady birdwatcher named in honour of one of my favourite quotes ever heard on a birding outing (*see* OUTINGS).

Many years ago, as a group of birders got back on the bus somewhere near Wilson's Promontory, a chirpy voice rang out (and you have to read this next bit out in your best Miss Marple English accent to get the best effect), 'Buntie, Buntie! Did you see the flame-tails?'

To this day, no one is exactly sure what she meant by 'flame-tails'. We suspect she may have seen a Red-browed Finch (or Firetail as it was then known). Or perhaps she had encountered a Flame Robin. Both were equally likely to have occurred at 'the Prom' in winter. But then again, she may have been referring to something with no red in the tail whatsoever, as Bunties tend not to be known for their identification skills.

But there is no shame in being a Buntie. For though they often see fewer birds than other birders (a group of Bunties chirping amongst themselves as they make their way through the bush is as noisy as a flock of lorikeets descending on a flowering gum), they are always incredibly enthusiastic and full of fun. And more than one tour leader has confessed to quite liking taking a group of Bunties out as the guide can show them the same birds time after time and they are always thrilled, thinking they are seeing them for the first time. And unlike some other birding types, they are particularly generous and always have a thermos of tea and some yummy cakes on hand to share with anyone that comes by.

Call / a generic term for the vocal sound emitted by a bird.

Calls can range from the harmonious, cascading song of the White-throated Gerygone to the guttural rattling of a Black-browed Albatross which sounds like straining, constipated sheep with laryngitis. The call of a Mallee Emu-wren can be so delicately high-pitched that anyone over the age of 40 struggles to hear it, whereas when I once had a Noisy Scrub-bird calling close to me I thought my ears were going to bleed.

When I am out birding in the bush, I reckon that almost 80 per cent of the birds that go down in my notebook I have identified by their call – sometimes more. If you can hear a bird you can usually track it down, but if you did it for every bird that called you would not get more than 50 metres from the car.

Seeing birds is always a highlight, but generally it is satisfactory simply to hear them. This means, of course, that you have to learn their calls. Often this is far more tricky than learning to identify them visually. This is one area where the field guides aren't of much use to you. I know what a Singing Honeyeater sounds like when I hear it, having heard this common dry country bird on countless occasions. 'Singing' is certainly a misnomer, but I'll be buggered if I could accurately describe it for you. This doesn't stop the authors of the field guides trying. Though one of the best descriptions I have come across is 'dry "*prrit, prrit, prrit*", running, machine-like "*crik,-crikit-crikit-crikit*"', reading it makes me completely forget what a Singing Honeyeater actually sounds like. Often those with no prior bird knowledge are the ones to best nail how a bird sounds. The books' descriptions of a Little Wattlebird call as being 'squeaky', 'raucous' or a 'guttural *yekkop, yekkop*' pale in comparison to a non-birding friend who once asked what the 'Swinging Safari' bird was. One of the calls of the Little Wattlebird is indeed just like the main phrase from that cheesy 1960s instrumental, 'A Swingin' Safari'.

The best way to learn a bird's call is to actually see the bird calling or to go into the bush with an experienced birder who can name the calls. Listening to recordings also helps. Once you know the calls, you will be amazed at how birding opens up to you. Of course, it's like learning any language – your skills can get rusty quite quickly. The first time I am back in a habitat I haven't been to for a while, it takes me a while to tune my ear as I refamiliarise myself with the calls.

That is assuming that it is a bird making a call in the first place. Some of the non-avian noises that I have mistaken for bird calls before include: dogs, cats, babies, tree branches rubbing on a tin roof, squeaky windmills, and birdwatching companions' burping, wheezing, rumbling and farting.

And, of course, the man-made sound that's most likely to be confused with a bird is a recording of the bird itself. Two friends of mine once called each other in using a tape while spotlighting in a rainforest, each thinking the other was an owl as they slowly crept up on each other. I recently did some fieldwork with a guy who had a Brown Treecreeper call for a ringtone. Even though we were working out in a coastal saltmarsh where there were no trees whatsoever, I was looking around for a tree every time he got an incoming call.

ACTION: By far the most comprehensive bird call tapes are the series produced by BOCA. They have recently converted them to CD for easier use. For more details try their website **www.birdobservers.org.au**

Camouflage / the means by which something renders itself indistinguishable from its surrounds.

Birds use their plumage to camouflage themselves. The Tawny Frogmouth blends imperceptibly into the dead branch it is sitting on. This is described as adopting a cryptic posture. Humans generally rely on their clothing for camouflage; whenever the city-based politician tours the country regions, he immediately swaps suit and tie for an Akubra hat and moleskin trousers. This is described as adopting a tragic posture.

Some birders are so into camouflage that they won't go out into the field with people who are wearing a particular colour such as red or white. Muted tones do make you more inconspicuous, but I suspect the camouflage thing is a bit overrated. After all, birds see the world in different hues to us, particularly when it comes to the ultraviolet end of the spectrum, so that nifty camouflaged hunting vest may, from the bird's perspective, actually be standing out like the proverbial. All that tut-tutting is probably doing more to drive the birds away than any loud clothing.

Having seen plenty of good birds in my street clothes, I suspect that what really matters are your movements when out birding. You can be so decked out in jungle greens as to be rendered invisible and it won't make a lick of difference if you are flailing about like Peter Garrett being electrocuted.

I believe the real reason birders like to dress in camouflage is that deep down we all harbour a secret desire to be the hunter-warrior type (and if you have seen the average weedy twitcher, you'll understand why we don't have many other outlets for such macho displays). After all, birdwatching is really just hunting without killing. It is battle for wimps. Birdwatchers even look as though they are dressed for battle. When you're kitted out in fatigues, and loaded up with heavy optical equipment, it's not much of a stretch to act out a John Wayne fantasy. Instead of storming the beaches, birders storm sewage farms. If Robert Duvall's character in *Apocalypse Now* had been a twitcher, he would have said, 'I love the smell of sewage in the morning. It's the smell of rarity.'

Even the way twitchers talk makes birdwatching sound like conquest. You don't see a new bird, you *have* it. You don't wander about in a place looking for a bird, you *burn up* or *flog* the habitat. Because birding is by its nature a gentle and quiet pastime, birdwatchers have to overcompensate. And if you don't believe that, go out birdwatching with a carload of twitchers. There is more bristling testosterone there than you'll find in a locker room full of rugby players.

Captain Twitchpants / an alpha male bristling with testosterone, this is a bloke who has typically come to birding a little later in life and is hell-bent on making up for lost time.

Not for the Captain the patient development and nurturing of birding knowledge, he explodes onto the scene, at any stage from his early 30s on, charging in and shaking things up. He certainly brings enormous enthusiasm for his newfound passion, which, however, is all too often at the expense of commonsense and established wisdom, for Captain Twitchpants thinks he knows it all. Often great company and a fabulous energiser of those around him, the main problem with Captain Twitchpants is that he ends up wasting a lot of people's time. Because he is too impatient or lacks empathy, he can't learn from the experience of others. The kind of guy who can't recognise an idea unless he thinks he has had it, he is the one who runs the dinghy aground on a sandbar because he claims he can see a passageway through the shallows to a place where there is bound to be loads of birds. He is the one who will organise a Night Parrot expedition to an area where it hasn't been seen since 1863, because no one else has known how to look properly for them the way he reckons he can. It is the Captain who will suggest, within minutes of a bird not showing where it is supposed to be, that the group try somewhere else, usually a place that people have been checking out for years without success. But because Captain Twitchpants lives in the now – primarily *his* now – he will go there anyway.

The Captain is likely to make more than his fair share of ID mistakes, due to over-enthusiasm and impatience with thorough research. But I don't know whether the Captain could be labelled a true stringer (*see* STRINGER), for he won't waste too much time defending his cock-ups; he'll already be onto the next bird, the next theory, the next adventure.

Checklist / a list of birds that enables birders to tick off the birds they have seen; also *see* LIST.

If everybody kept their own checklist, then individual variations would be inevitable and it would become impossible to compare like against like. Some people may only include mainland Australia, others will add all the overseas territories. Some may consider the Western Bowerbird a full species, others may see it as only a sub-species of Spotted Bowerbird. For this reason I endorse the idea of one national, uniform checklist, setting out an objective standard everyone can refer to.

The checklist that currently holds most credence amongst the general birding populace is the one produced for Birds Australia by Les Christidis and Walter Boles. Originally published as far back as 1994, they have been working ever since to produce a new one, but it is taking longer than expected, due to the changes in bird taxonomy, particularly in light of recent DNA sequencing advances (*see* TAXONOMY). The new checklist is supposed to have come out 'next year' for the past ten years, which is a bit like saying the war will be over by Christmas – true as long as you don't specify which Christmas.

Birders, particularly those that keep a life list, are waiting with bated breath for the new checklist, for if any current species are 'lumped' (combined with another species) or 'split' (a former subspecies being separated out as a distinct species), some people may drop a few species while others will potentially gain a whole swag of armchair ticks (*see* ARMCHAIR TICKS). When the checklist does come out, the twitching masses will be gathered like journalists after a budget lockdown, scrambling to pore over the new document.

Inevitably, a few birders will scoff at the arrogant presumption of the compilers of the new checklist – how dare they dictate what I can and can't tick off on my list? I'd rather be strung up by my privates and have electrodes attached to my nipples than ever recognise Tasmanian Scrubwren as a full species! I am always wary of the arguments of those who dismiss the views of the 'so-called experts' out of hand. To me, 'so-called expert' is merely code for an expert you happen not to agree with, just as you can guarantee that someone proclaiming to speak of 'the true facts' essentially means 'not facts but my opinion, which is contrary to the established facts'.

I figure that the decisions taken by the checklist makers are probably based on scientific evidence slightly better researched than my limited subjective experience, so even if I don't agree with every decision taken, I can live with them. There are undoubtedly things that the ordinary birder knows that the scientific community isn't up to speed on, but for now, I'll happily follow whatever the 'official' checklist determines so that at least I will be singing from the same songbook as the majority of the birding community. And who knows, maybe come the next one, there will be more splits for birds I have seen than lumps.

Chooks / 1. birds that Australians colloquially call chickens. 2. birds that Aussie twitchers colloquially call common birds, that is, birds they have already seen.

Oddly enough, in the world of the twitcher a chook is not a chook. There are two species of chicken on the Australian bird list, both descendants of captive birds gone wild. The Red Junglefowl, our domestic chook which originated in South-East Asia, is tickable on some of the Barrier Reef islands, and on Norfolk, Christmas and Cocos (Keeling) Islands. The Green Junglefowl is the Javan cousin of the Red and a feral population exists in the Cocos (Keeling) Islands in the far-flung Indian Ocean. Most Australians have never set foot on the Cocos. Most hard-core twitchers have, specifically to see the chook, which is anything but a chook.

Climate change / as those altruistic battlers from the fossil fuel industry (the poor dears are down to their last couple of hundred billion) keep telling us, human-induced climate change is nothing but a myth pushed by those fat cat scientists and climatologists of the rapacious climate change industry.

But suppose that climate change was real. How might it affect Australia's bird population?

The truth is, it's hard to know at this stage. As with all massive changes to an ecosystem, there will be many, many losers, but a few species will probably do rather well out of it. Already we are seeing a movement south of many east-coast rainforest species such as Channel-billed Cuckoo, Common Koel, White-headed Pigeon and Figbird. This is likely to be due to climate change, but the evidence is complicated by other factors such as the spread of weed species like Privet and Camphor Laurel, which some of these species have learned to feed on.

The real disaster is looming for birds which are restricted to mountain-tops, for their homes, already remnants from colder times, will start to shrink and they will be stranded on ever-diminishing islands of suitable habitat. At first glance, this doesn't seem to be too much of a problem for Australian birds, as there are no endemic species restricted solely to the high country of the south-east, although the Black Currawong of Tasmania could be a contender. But most people forget that there is an entire suite of birds that's largely restricted to the upland rainforests of North Queensland: this group includes Lesser Sooty Owl, Fernwren, Mountain Thornbill, Bridled Honeyeater, Grey-headed Robin and Golden Bowerbird. A change of climate will make the habitat unsuitable for these upland specialists, as it is most likely that more lowland plant species will begin to shift upwards and take over.

Across the country other changes, perhaps not as dramatic but far-reaching nonetheless, will be occurring. Though it can't be conclusively proven that the decade-long drought over the southern half of the country is part of human-induced climate change, the consensus is that droughts are likely to become both more frequent and more severe. Not a good forecast for those woodland species that have already been doing it tough. And the same goes for many of our wetland species, which are rapidly running out of wetlands.

However it pans out, birdwatching in Australia will be quite a different proposition in 100 or even 50 years time.

Couple / a rather rare occurrence amongst bird-nerds.

Birding couples aren't all that common, but sometimes a partner finally relents and joins in with the other's hobby. This can lead to a lifetime of fulfilment, or – given that birdwatching can be a deceptively competitive pastime – can lead to all sorts of tensions. Things can get very sticky indeed if one partner gets to see a species (particularly a crippler – *see* CRIPPLER) and the other doesn't.

Interestingly, on a website devoted to listing birders' totals, there was not one birding couple in which the woman had seen more than the man. In more than one case the difference between them was only a solitary species, and it was always the husband who had seen that extra one, not the wife. I'm not saying men are more competitive and hate to lose – well maybe I am – but I wonder how those extra ticks were obtained. Did he sneak out in the middle of the night to nab a Marbled Frogmouth? Did his 'night out with the boys' at the strip club mask an intention to go spotlighting for a Sooty Owl? Or did he conveniently suppress that Letter-winged Kite he saw perched on a roadside tree when they were driving to Birdsville?

What I would really love to know is what happens if the woman manages to get a bigger list than her partner. Does he feel as emasculated as those traditional men whose wives earn a higher salary sometimes feel? And in the event of a divorce, who gets custody of the list?

Cox's Sandpiper / one of the great controversies of Australian birding relates to this bird that wasn't.

When a couple of odd-looking waders were seen in the 1960s is was at first claimed they were Dunlin, a Northern Hemisphere wader that had never been seen here before. When further investigation throughout the 1970s led to them being declared a hitherto undescribed species, a bunfight erupted as to what to call it, with Cox's Sandpiper eventually winning out. The only trouble was, it was suspected at the time and later proved through DNA analysis that these birds weren't a distinct species at all but a hybrid between two other wader species, the Curlew and Pectoral Sandpipers.

It may sound all rather dry but at the time the Cox's Sandpiper saga was played out with a level of passion and vitriol that one would associate with a soap opera. In fact, the scenario was so highly charged that it was picked up by the scriptwriters of the most popular soap of the time, *Dallas*. Here is a hitherto unreleased transcript of the episode:

Bobby Ewing (played by Patrick Duffy) enters an executive bird hide to discover JR Ewing (a pre-liver transplant Larry Hagman) looking out over a wetland laughing in the manner of a pantomime villain.

BOBBY: What have you done this time, JR?

JR: Me? Why I just discovered a new species of bird – I'm going to call it Cox's Sandpiper!

BOBBY: Why, you lowdown coyote, JR, I believe that I have the naming rights to that bird, and I aims to call it . . . False Dunlin!

JR: Too late, Bobby, I've already registered the name, so Cox's Sandpiper it is.

BOBBY: False Dunlin! You son of a . . .

JR: Cox's!

Bobby: False Dunlin!

JR: Cox's!

They pull out revolvers and are about to shoot each other when Pam Barnes Ewing (played by Victoria Principal before weird things happened to her face) rushes in between them.

VICTORIA: Boys, boys, stop all this fussin' and a-fightin'. I've just come back from the lab, and that sandpiper ain't neither a False Dunlin nor a Cox's Sandpiper! It's a hybrid. The Mummy was as Curlew Sandpiper. And the Daddy was ... you, JR!

Bobby puts his hand to his head in disbelief.

BOBBY: I hope this is all just another dream.

JR puts his hand to his gut in pain.

JR: Ooh, there goes my liver. Oh well, plenty more where that came from.

TRANSCRIPT ENDS.

Interestingly, since it was confirmed that it was only a hybrid and taken off the official Australian list, the number of reports of Cox's Sandpiper-type birds has fallen off. This could be due to natural causes – the two species that hybridise only have a small area where their breeding ranges overlap and may not have had the opportunity to mate too often – but the more likely explanation is that because it is no longer tickable, birders are far less likely to look for it, or report it once they have found it.

Crippler / any highly sought-after species of rare bird; of British origin, the word probably derives from the notion that some birds are so staggeringly amazing that a twitcher is rooted to the spot, 'crippled' with awe, upon seeing one.

A Galah, though a delightful bird, is not a crippler, because they occur in flocks of thousands and their range is extensive. A Red-capped Parrot may seem like a crippler for someone birding south-west Australia for the first time, but as it is not uncommon in its restricted range it is technically not a crippler. A Night Parrot, on the other hand, would not be a mere crippler, it would be more like a total incapacitator, leaving the person who saw it quadriplegic, apoplectic and needing to be fed through a straw.

Paradoxically, it is the twitcher who doesn't get the crippler who feels the pain.

Dead cert / the one term that you should never, ever utter when out birding, when you're about to go birding, or even when thinking about birding.

I am not one for superstition in any form, but whomsoever declares that a bird is a 'dead cert' is doomed to walk the earth as a zombie. Not the undead, brain-eating type of zombie, but the kind that walks around in circles for hours and hours in a futile search for a bird that, as you tell your increasingly sceptical birdwatching companions, was seen by someone else only yesterday.

I learnt about dead certs the hard way ten years ago on a twitchathon (*see* TWITCHATHON), which has become known amongst our team as The Great Hooded Robin Debacle. Three days before the Twitchathon, in an isolated patch of bush, we found not one but six Hooded Robins, including a pair on a nest with two eggs. Anticipating that even the mightiest of robin parents couldn't successfully hatch and raise a brood in a few days, Hooded Robin was ascribed 'dead cert' status.

Naturally, on the day there was no sign of the eggs, the parents or any of the other Hooded Robins. It was as if the birding gods smote them from the Earth as punishment for our hubris.

So let this be a warning to the optimistic beginner. Birds have a mind of their own, and wings to boot, so anything is possible. Even if you have seen a magpie in your back yard every day for the last ten years, the moment you declare it a dead cert, particularly to somebody that you have promised to show a magpie to, is the moment that the magpie will fail to put in an appearance.

Dip / the most dreaded term in the twitching vocabulary; to miss out on a bird that you have been looking for; also known as dipping out.

You know that feeling you have when you are lying all snug and tucked up in bed on a cold morning and you hear the rumbling of the garbage truck outside, as you realise that you haven't put the rubbish out? That sinking despair in the pit of your stomach as the truck passes your house and you are left standing barefoot in your pyjamas, holding a bin overflowing with festering junk – that is exactly what it feels like to dip out on a rare bird.

It's not such a great drama if you dip out on that rosella you normally see in the local park, but if you've flown across the country for a Black-tailed Gull only to be told that it hasn't been seen since Thursday, then dipping can throw you into a near-suicidal, existential crisis.

And yes, that was me I was using in that example. Australia's third Black-tailed Gull, had turned up in Townsville, North Queensland. As the only two previous Australian sightings had been more than twenty years earlier, this was definitely one that I needed to unblock (*see* BLOCKERS). I was unable to exercise my fast twitch muscles and had to wait a week before I could go for it (*see* FAST-TWITCH MUSCLES). I rang a birding contact in Townsville who said the bird had been seen on the Thursday. It was now lunchtime Saturday. The first flight to north Queensland wasn't until the next morning and so at dawn I duly flew the length of the country to look for the bird. There was no sign of it. Another birder arrived, and asked, 'You haven't come up from Melbourne for this, have you? The bird hasn't been seen since Thursday!' The addition of that one word – *since* – would have saved me from one of the biggest dips in Australian twitching history, not to mention an $800 airfare.

Not that it was the greatest dip ever; that title undoubtedly belongs to the twitcher who dipped on Australia's first Rosy Starling. Twice. After a Rosy Starling was seen out on the plains near Broome, this particular twitcher was the first to arrive on the scene, having flown across the county at a moment's notice. The starling was a no-show. A few days later, the starling turned up again at the same location. I went for it, as did another Melbourne twitcher. After a nervous day's wait we finally saw the bird. Unlike other vagrants, which are often bedraggled and dull, this bird was a real cutie in a pink-and-black combination that wouldn't look out of place on a Paris catwalk (*see* VAGRANT). While we were enjoying the bird, our unlucky twitching friend was somewhere in north Queensland, unable to get to Broome immediately. Eventually he changed his flights and flew from Townsville via Cairns and Darwin to Broome. When he finally arrived in Broome, the bird was gone, this time for good.

After flying the equivalent of Sydney to London he had double-dipped on the Rosy Starling. And in birdwatching, just as at a swank party, nobody likes a double dip.

Dipfearia / a psychological condition that arises when a birder fears that they are going to miss out on seeing a bird.

Dipfearia's primary symptoms – high pulse rate, sweaty palms, tightness of breath, feeling of paranoia – though they closely mimic the symptoms displayed by a heavy amphetamine abuser, are usually not harmful in themselves. It is dipfearia's secondary effects that are the most dangerous to the health of the sufferer: driving too long through the night in order to get to where the rare bird was last seen; staying out in the wet and the dark, hoping the rare owl comes back to the perch it landed in when somebody saw it three nights before; sticking a hand in a burrow that is just as likely to contain a sleeping Tiger Snake as it does a nesting Little Shearwater. Ultimately though, it is the companions of the sufferer who really pay the price – the children whose holidays are spent sitting in the car waiting for Dad to flog that patch of habitat one more time in order to get tickable views of the Nullarbor Quail-thrush; the wife whose notions of a romantic honeymoon on a tropical island are blown out of the water when her new partner spends most of his time lurking around the Christmas Island rubbish tip, and the grandmother whose twitching grandson wanders off during his grandfather's funeral because he thought he heard a Swift Parrot feeding in the nearby trees. Sadly, despite the best efforts of researchers at The Big Twitch Institute, there is still no known cure for Dipfearia.

Dowitcher / a type of wader with one of the more ridiculous names in the bird world.

The Dowitcher is not actually named after a withered Chinese Empress, but is in fact a Native American (possibly Mohawk) word for a 'snipe'. Not that we see the American species here too often – there've been only two records of the Short-billed Dowitcher to date. Even the Asian Dowitcher, a regular visitor, is no easy get. While the odd bird is reported along the Queensland coast, it is only around Broome that they are reliably seen, and then only in small numbers.

I have seen the Asian Dowitcher in Australia but not the Short-billed Yankee version. I tried. I went for the only twitchable one, a single bird that was found at the Price Saltworks, a couple of hours north of Adelaide. After driving from Melbourne I found two flocks of birds which could be harbouring a Yankee Dowitcher. As I settled down to scan through one, a local birder purporting to be an expert came by with a group. He confidently proclaimed that I was looking in the wrong place as the Dowitcher had only been seen where the other flock was. Bowing to his local knowledge I followed him and his party. Despite extensive scanning through the flock no Dowitcher could be found. I watched as the original flock wheeled into flight and headed off towards their low-tide feeding grounds on the Gulf of St Vincent, a distinctly Dowitcher-shaped silhouette amongst them.

It turns out the expert was no such thing. He had only been to see the Dowitcher once before and was pontificating on the basis of this limited information. Essentially I had dipped on the Short-billed Dowitcher because I had been taken in by a duffer (*see* DIP, DUFFER).

Dude / a generally disparaging term used by birders for non-birders; as in, 'I went out to Inskip Point but there were too many dudes around to have any chance of seeing the Black-breasted Button-quail'.

The dude moniker is most pointed when it is directed at another birdwatcher, as it implies a general softness or wimpiness. Gung-ho birders like to take pride in the discomfort they will endure and will readily denigrate anyone who fails to live up to their Spartan approach as being a dude, even if that involves eminently sensible choices like sleeping in a real bed as opposed to in the car or on the ground; or stopping to eat a proper meal rather than eating soggy, month-old muesli bars on the go.

Nearly all of us exhibit dudish tendencies at some point or other, so there is no real shame in being a dude. In case you're wondering where you fit in on the dude spectrum, opposite is a rough guide.

If you identify with two or more statements from the first column, chances are you have dudish tendencies and may even – shock, horror – get some enjoyment out of your birdwatching.

If any one of the statements from the second column have you nodding in agreement, you can rest assured that you are not a dude. There is a good chance, however, that you are neurotic, obsessive and so highly strung that you can't ever really enjoy yourself when birding.

Dude	Hard-core birder
I possess a lilo or air mattress for sleeping rough.	Gravel is my lilo.
When tired while driving to see a bird, I stop and have a powernap.	When tired, I wind down the window, fuel up on caffeine and energy drinks, and slap myself in the face to stay awake in order to get to a bird before it flies off.
I won't go out birding if the weather is too rough.	I will only go out birding if the weather is rough – it is my best chance of finding a storm-blown seabird.
If I haven't seen a bird after an hour's searching, I will give up.	If I haven't seen a bird after ten hour's searching I conclude that the original claim was clearly dodgy.
I will only chase a lifer if it is within a day's drive (see LIFER).	I will only not chase a lifer if I am on life support, and even then, if I can fit the ventilator into the car, I'll give it a crack.
I like to sleep in.	I like to sleep in the tops of rainforest trees because it gives me a better chance of seeing birds first thing in the morning.

Duffer / a character who is quite often very cheery and pleasant company but is basically a fairly ordinary, if not downright incompetent, bird-watcher.

Not that he will think so; for the duffer is always blissfully unaware of just what a duffer he really is. Oddly enough, duffers are generally men. I have often found that your typical duffer is somebody in a fairly high-powered position in the workforce or an expert in another field who is used to being deferred to and not having his opinion questioned. Thus, there seem to be quite a few doctors, lawyers, captains of industry, and academics who fall into the duffer category.

Once out at Werribee Sewage Farm I bumped into a former lecturer who had given me quite a bit of grief while I was at university (no doubt justified, because I was rather slack, though that didn't excuse his supercilious manner towards me). When I asked the carload of birders he was with if anything was about, he answered for them (for the duffer is a duffer as much for his willingness to expose himself as a duffer as he is for any duffer actions). Some of the claims he made appeared rather dubious to me, so I plied him for more details on one of them, a Lesser Sand Plover, as it is rather unusual at Werribee. He was adamant, telling me in a dismissive tone that it clearly was a Lesser Sand Plover because it didn't have the large bill and long legs of a Greater Sand Plover. It didn't either, because it was in fact a Double-banded Plover, which is seen far more at Werribee than either the Greater or the Lesser Sand Plover.

He wasn't a duffer because he had misidentified the bird; he was a duffer because he had so pompously fobbed off any suggestions that it could be something else. Duffers are the kind of people who are constantly hoisting themselves on their own petards; standing a in field saying, 'Oh, you never

ever get Singing Bushlarks here,' at the precise moment that a Singing Bushlark hops up on a fence post and starts singing its heart out.

Warning: While you need to be wise to the duffer, ignore them completely at your own peril lest you become the duffer. The exact moment you dismiss out of hand a duffer's reported sighting will be the only time he is ever on the money.

Duff gen / birder's term for poor information, particularly information relating to where to find a particular species.

'Gen' is, I believe, a British term for information, and 'duff' I am sure must come from duffer; certainly a lot of bad gen emanates from the mouths of duffers (*see* DUFFER).

Duff gen is not a good thing. There is nothing more frustrating to turn up somewhere expecting to find a bird and discovering you have been given duff gen – the bird is not actually where you were told it would be, or worse, it is not even the species it was reported to be.

Egg collectors / the collection of the eggs of wild birds, sometimes given the dubious name 'oology' so as to lend this rapacious pastime a veneer of scientific credibility.

This pastime introduced a lot of birders of a certain age to birdwatching. Happily, it is a thing of the past – almost. Though not as prevalent as in some other countries, it would be naïve in the extreme to believe that egg-snatching, and the equally odious bird-smuggling, don't happen here. The smuggling of endangered species or more common birds such as our parrots and cockatoos that fetch a good price on the overseas markets is a lucrative trade, decimating populations of wild birds in South America and Africa. There is no reason to presume it doesn't happen here.

This is why birders should be very wary in publicising details of sightings of rare birds, particularly when they are nesting. In fact it is never advisable to give information about specific nest sites to anyone who does not need to know, although exceptions could be land managers or rangers if the site is in a conservation reserve, and landholders whose ploughing, spraying or burning off may impact on nesting birds. It may go against the grain, but you should seriously consider whether to tell other birders, as the extra attention around the nest site may spook the parent birds, causing them to abandon their nest, not to mention the danger from animal and human predators. If there are egg collectors out there, the chances are their information networks will have alerted them to the presence of the nest long before a birder found it, but it is a good idea to exercise caution (*see* ETHICAL BIRDWATCHING).

Ego / the inflation of one's self-esteem into a state of self-conceit; somebody who is up themselves.

I was introduced to the term ego through the Skyhooks song, 'Ego is not a Dirty Word'. Being seven at the time, I assumed that ego must in fact be a dirty word, and began using it in the playground as a term of abuse: 'Stop hogging the swing, you stupid ego-head!' It was years until I learnt what ego really meant.

Readers may suspect I still don't, as surely birdwatching, being a gentle pastime with the focus on the birds, couldn't possibly involve rampant egos? Wrong. What most people don't realise is that, for many birders, birdwatching is their life, that which defines them. They judge others (and themselves) purely on the criteria of their birding skills. The birder driven by ego doesn't go birding to discover an objective truth (the identity of a species). They grab the binoculars in a quest to prove their own self-worth.

Everyone has a tendency to boast. After finding a rare bird or nailing a difficult identification puzzle, there is a natural inclination to feel good about yourself, but where you can tell a true birding egotist is when they offer up an interesting sighting they have had. If they tell you, 'I had a Broad-billed Sandpiper down at the mudflats this morning,' and the emphasis is on the 'I' then you can be pretty sure they are telling you, not so much because they want you to know that there is a rare wader in the area, but that they were the person clever enough to find it.

Another way to gauge the levels of ego in a fellow birder is if you are the one telling them about the Broad-billed Sandpiper. If they are genuinely interested about the bird being there, they will seek details of the circumstances so that they can also hopefully see this crippler (*see* CRIPPLER), or even if they have no intention of going for the bird, they still find your sighting interesting. If they are more interested in themselves, they will seek details of the circumstances so that they can hopefully prove you wrong, thereby demonstrating their superior birding skills. Either that or they may gazump you with stories of how they saw four Broad-billed Sandpipers at the same site the week before.

The story of the multiple sightings of Broad-billed Sandpiper may or may not be true because the ego-driven personality is also one of the most likely candidates to be a convincing stringer – their need to come out on top overriding their desire to be accurate (*see* STRINGER).

Emu / an Australian endemic bird (*see* ENDEMIC) that appears on our national coat of arms with the kangaroo, supposedly because both are the only animals that cannot take a backward step.

It is a great idea that suits Australia's idea of our national character (we won't back down, Australia is always advancing and so on), but I have difficulty believing that the Emu can't really take a backward step.

So I have made it my life's mission to determine this question. Whenever I see an Emu, I block its path to see whether I can force it into a backward step. Luckily the Emu doesn't have the deadly sharp claws of its relative the cassowary – which is capable of disembowelling an adult human – but by jingoes, they still can pack quite a kick. The bruising lasts for weeks!

Endemic / a species of bird that is confined to one region or country.

Australia has around 330 endemic species, depending on who you listen to or what checklist you follow. If you include the birds that Australia shares with New Guinea, that number rises substantially. Whichever list you go by, this is still a large number, probably second only to Indonesia, and certainly one of the highest proportions of endemics of any country in the world. Each state (except Victoria) has its own endemics, which are, of course, Australian endemics. Thus the Rock Warbler, which is found only near Sydney, is both a NSW and Australian endemic.

Australia is also host to quite a number of endemic bird families such as the lyrebirds, scrub-birds, the Plains-wanderers and the Minogues. Recent scientific research indicates that virtually all of the world's songbirds, including crows, nightingales and starlings, like Kylie Minogue, had their origins in Australia before they were exported to the rest of the world.

The fact that we have so many endemics means that there is no one else to blame if we drop the ball on them and let them die out. Politicians are always banging on about Aussie values; well, you can't get much more uniquely Australian than a Superb Lyrebird or a Spotted Quail-thrush or a Grey Grasswren all of which originated here. How Aussie's that?

Ethical birdwatching / birding in such a manner that (a) doesn't harm the bird or its environment, (b) doesn't harm other birders and their enjoyment of watching birds and (c) doesn't harm other people or their livelihoods.

In terms of threats to birds, the activities of birdwatchers would not figure particularly high up on the list. Birding is going to pose far less of a hindrance to a bird than habitat destruction, hunting, pollution, extreme weather, collision with vehicles and buildings, feral animals and a million other things that can ruin a bird's day. But there is no denying that the activity of birdwatchers can have an impact on the birds they are trying to watch. By ethical birding, I am not necessarily talking about wearing rope shoes and only eating fallen fruit when you are out looking at birds, but being aware of the potential impacts that your actions can have. As a birder you have to ask yourself constantly whether seeing the bird is more important than its comfort and safety.

You would hope that even the most ardent ticker (*see* TICKER) would agree that the interests of the bird come first. But when you are desperate to see a bird, in the heat of the battle, where would you draw the line? Here is a hypothetical situation that illustrates just such a situation.

You have always wanted to see a Plains-wanderer, a quail-like bird that is only found in the dry inland grasslands of south-eastern Australia. You have travelled a long way to see this bird and may never be back in the area again. You have searched fruitlessly for a week, and on your last afternoon you see a possible Plains-wanderer briefly fly up and disappear into a large paddock. Knowing that these birds are very cryptic and will almost never flush again, what do you do?

a. Sit and wait quietly for the Plains-wanderer to miraculously fly back up – something it hasn't done all week – all the while hoping that you don't breathe out too heavily lest you exhale too much carbon dioxide in which case you'd have to buy some more carbon credits to cover the greenhouse emissions of your trip.

b. Wait until night and spotlight the bird because you know that they are less wary at night, and less likely to be seen by predators if you flush it (of course, you will be using a filter over the lens of your spotlight so as not to startle the bird – *see* SPOTLIGHTING).

c. Walk slowly through the paddock to where the bird landed with the slim hope that you might see it without disturbing it again.

d. Run as quickly as possible to the spot because you know that Plains-wanderers never flush twice and it will simply disappear if you don't act straightaway.

e. Set fire to the paddock – that'll make the little bastard show!

I assume most people will probably answer somewhere between B and D. Exactly where you draw the line will depend on the values that you have already packed along with your field guide, sun hat and gaiters. If you feel the moral answer is clearly A, that is well and good, but in all honesty, you are probably by definition not birdwatching. You are bird *notwatching*. You are bird *just knowing the bird is there is good enough for me-ing*. The very act of entering a bird's habitat is going to affect the bird in some way, however small. The ethical question confronting every birder is how far should we take that level of disturbance before it outweighs our desire for an encounter with a bird?

And what of our duty to other birders? In the next hypothetical imagine that on the other side of that same paddock is another birdwatcher whom you know has been looking just as desperately for Plains-wanderer as you. What would your preferred course of action be?

a. Yell or signal to him that you have just seen a potential Plains-wanderer, even though it will probably spook the bird so that neither of you will see it.

b. Try and see the bird first and hope that he will be able to see from your activity that you are onto something and will come over.

c. Try and see the bird first and then tell him as soon as is possible about the bird (though this puts you in danger of gripping him off – *see* GRIPPING OFF).

d. Try and see the bird first, and then do not tell him about it because you know that you and he are on level pegging with your life lists and Plains-wanderer will put you one up (*see* LIFE LISTS).

e. Set fire to the paddock and hope that the flames flush the bird while the smoke blinds your rival so that he can't see it.

And there may be non-birders to consider. What if the paddock the Plains-wanderer was seen on was private property? Would you:

a. Already have sought permission to enter from the owner to make sure it was OK.

b. Go off and try to find the owner to get permission to enter.

c. Jump the fence and worry about permission later.

    d. Jump the fence even though you had already sought permission and the owner had said no.

    e. Jump the fence, set fire to the paddock and let it burn into his adjacent paddocks too because the lousy mongrel wouldn't give you permission to enter in the first place.

And finally, there are the personal ethics of the twitcher. If that fleeting glimpse is all you got of the bird, do you add it to your list?

    a. No, because I didn't see it well enough.

    b. No, I wouldn't count it for my life list but I would count it for my year list or state list, which I have less strict standards for.

    c. Yes, I would count it as a Plains-wanderer because they are meant to be in this area so that it is probably what it was (*see* STRINGER).

    d. Yes, I would count it as a Plains-wanderer because when I got home later and looked at my photos of the paddock I could see a Plains-wanderer hiding in the grass so I must have seen one, even if I didn't notice at the time (*see* ARMCHAIR TICKS).

    e. Yes, I would count it, and I would set fire to the paddock (*see* A PSYCHOLOGIST BECAUSE BOY HAVE YOU GOT ISSUES, BUDDY).

All this just from a brief glimpse of a bird. And you thought birding was a simple hobby.

External territories / the bits of Australia whose birds aren't generally regarded as part of the Australian avifauna (*see* AVIFAUNA) but make it onto the list by quirks of history and politics; includes Christmas and Cocos-Keeling Islands in the tropical Indian Ocean (and Ashmore Reef too, I guess), Heard and Macquarie Islands in the Southern Ocean, and Norfolk and Lord Howe Islands in the Pacific.

Most Australians know or care little for the external territories. In fact the Howard Government excised them from Australia for the purposes of immigration with barely a whimper from the general populace. However, if any of these territories, especially Christmas Island, were to be invaded by a foreign power, twitchers would probably be the first in line to volunteer to take up arms to take them back. An army of angry, anoraked Asbirders, now that's a scary thought that would have our enemies quaking in their boots.

The reason the territories are so well regarded by twitchers is that they offer a whole bunch of free extra ticks for their Australian lists. Well, not quite for nothing, as it costs an arm and a leg to get to most of these places. But for twitchers it is worth it, because the territories not only have their own endemic species and nesting colonies of seabirds that are difficult to see in Australian waters, but those territories to the north also receive a fair share of overshooting Asian migrants which can really bump up the Aussie list (*see* OVERSHOOTING, ENDEMIC).

Fast-twitch muscles / 1. muscles that provide strength and speed for short periods of time. 2. muscles that provide the twitcher the strength of purpose to overcome commonsense, rationality and the objections of family members and employers in order to speed towards a rarity as soon as the twitcher hears about it.

Big Twitch Institute research reveals that in Australia the average stay of a crippler (*see* CRIPPLER) is 3.12 days. Some birds linger for much longer – our first Cape Gannet was discovered in Port Phillip Bay in 1981 and was still being ticked by birders some sixteen years later – but when a vagrant first makes an appearance, there is no guarantee it won't fly off the same day. As a general rule, the birders with the most active fast-twitch muscles are the ones that avoid dipping because they get to the site as quickly as possible.

Exercising the fast-twitch muscles doesn't automatically guarantee success. Like the athlete known for bursting too quickly out of the blocks, there is a higher chance of false starts. You may well arrive at your destination to find that the bird has flown, something you would have been fully aware of had you had waited for further confirmation. If the dash has just been across town, then dipping out is not so traumatic; if you have used up serious frequent-flyer points or booked on expensive last-minute interstate flights, it can be utter disaster.

What is even more maddening is if you finally arrive at your destination only to find out that the bird has been misidentified in the first instance, and is not quite the crippler you had been hoping for. Nearly every year there is at least one claim of an American Golden Plover somewhere in Australia, but you rarely get twitchers instantly racing after them as these birds can be so hard to tell from the more usual Pacific Golden Plover (one study in Alaska found that up to 15 per cent of them can't be told apart, even in the hand) that not until one turns up with a sworn affidavit from a noted Republic and is singing 'I'm a Yankee Doodle Plover' will a twitcher even think about going for it. There is no point wasting all that time, money and goodwill from those around you for a bird that isn't a new tick (*see* TICK) as did a birder who twice flew from Darwin to Melbourne for a Wilson's Phalarope, only to discover nothing but the similar looking (but relatively common) Marsh Sandpiper at the place where the phalarope was claimed to be (*see* DUFF GEN).

In my Big Twitch year I developed quite an advanced fast-twitch muscle that netted me some absolute cripplers such as Canada Goose, Blue-and-white Flycatcher and Isabelline Wheatear. My rapid responses also cost me a lot of unnecessary time for birds that ended up hanging around, such as the Kentish Plover, for which I made a crazed, eighteen-hour round trip when it would end up staying put for the following two months.

That one frenetic year seems to have worn out my fast-twitch muscle, however, as a recent tickable American Golden Plover turned up in Adelaide and I didn't rouse myself to go for it for almost three months. When I finally made the time, the saltworks it occupied were rendered inaccessible by an unseasonal downpour and I couldn't gain access. I still don't have a confirmed AGP on my list. Who knows when another tickable one may turn up?

Father / the male parent who often inspires a love of birds in their children. Or not.

Having a father who is interested in birds is how many birders get their start. This was certainly not the case with me. My dad was your typical knockabout Aussie bloke. He liked the footy, the cricket, the races and beer, and that, in many ways, was about it. He never really got my obsession for birdwatching, and he certainly thought that all my birdwatching friends were freaks.

I remember once at dinner when my mum was grilling me on why I never brought any girlfriends home for them to meet, my dad interrupted with, 'Yeah, are you a poofter or something?'

I rolled my eyes and responded, 'No Dad, I'm a birdwatcher.'

He paused, and as he took a sip of his beer, muttered to himself, 'Think I'd rather you were a poof.'

Over time his attitude mellowed and he came to appreciate some aspects of my birding. He loved the countryside and we did several short trips together – to Broken Hill, Victoria's Western District, King and Flinders Island – where we combined both our passions. I would leave him in the local pub while I went out birding. It was a match made in heaven.

My father died from lung cancer a few years ago, and in his final weeks when he was too breathless to be able to do much, he would sit and look out the window at the birds on the nearby lake. It brought him great peace. He even trained the local pelicans to come up to the back door to be fed (*see* FEEDING BIRDS). He had been around when I found the Bridled Tern (*see* FIRSTS), and though at the time his response to all the twitchers who descended on our home was to nick off to the pub to avoid 'those freaks', just before he died he told me proudly, 'You know what, Sean, I've seen a Bridled Tern in Victoria, how many people can say that?'

I knew then that at long last he had finally got something about my birdwatching.

Favourite bird / as a birder you will inevitably be asked what is your favourite bird. For a twitcher the answer is simple – the next new one.

When that answer doesn't suffice, you will have to come up with something. My usual fall-back is the Grey-crowned Babbler. I'm not sure whether it really is my favourite any more, but it was when I was first asked the question; the same way that I have never really updated my favourite film list, so things like Pink Floyd's *The Wall* and *Rocky III* probably still figure high on the list. I really must update that list.

The reason the Grey-crowned Babbler was up there was not only because they are a pretty groovy bird, always on the go in their family groups with the weird array of wild cries and chattering calls that led to their colloquial name, 'Yahoo', but also because of where I first got to know them. One of the last colonies of these birds in southern Victoria would hang around the playground of my high school. When I first went there I didn't know a soul and for much of the first year or so I was pretty miserable. Not that it was a cringingly awful Dickensian institutionalised misery, just your usual, it-takes-a-new-kid-a-while-to-completely-fit-in kind of miserable.

So at lunchtimes I would amuse myself by trying to follow the group of babblers around the school grounds, not an easy task as they were pretty active and I had to disguise my interest somewhat so that I didn't give the other kids fuel for another barrage of 'poofter' taunts.

That colony has now gone. Not just moved-up-the-road gone but disappeared-off-the face-of-the-Earth gone, as have all the other colonies in southern Victoria.

 ACTION: If you are feeling mischievous when another birder asks you what your favourite bird is, opt for a really common or (especially) introduced bird such as the Common Myna. As they try to fathom your decision, sit back and enjoy watching their brains almost explode. It is like saying to a Beatles aficionado that you think John was overrated and just rode on the coat-tails of Paul, who had all the real talent. It drives them nuts.

Feeding birds / providing food for wild birds.

Feeding wild birds has both positive and negative effects, with most of the positives on the human side of the equation. There is an exquisite thrill to be had from having a kookaburra take a piece of meat from your hand that few other activities in the modern world can match. Sure designer drugs, beta-blockers and chakra realignment will make you feel all right for a while, but how many of them will give a lasting beak-sized scar on your hand as a permanent reminder of your blissful experience?

Unfortunately for the birds, that free meal brings with it a whole swag of downsides, mainly because it interferes with a natural state of affairs. Feeding tends to favour the more aggressive species, such as magpies, mynas, wattlebirds and other large honeyeaters, those that can hold their own on the feeding tray, perpetuating a cycle where those species tend to thrive, often to the detriment of more timid species.

Another downside to feeding is that it can have consequences in the spread of avian diseases. If the feeding station is not regularly cleaned, the chances of a virus spreading between birds that would otherwise not come into contact with each other increases exponentially.

And there is little point feeding birds if you're supplying the wrong gear. Generally a bird won't eat what it isn't adapted to eat, so there is little point putting out seed and hoping a robin will drop by for a feed. And strangely enough, most people shy away from breeding mealworms, which are essentially a type of maggot, to bring the robins in. Many honeyeaters and lorikeets can be attracted with sugared water, but this is usually deficient in vital nutrients and is the avian equivalent of junk food.

Nectar-feeding species tend to be nomadic, following the blossom, so a regular supply of artificial nectar can keep the birds in the one location for too long. Such birds usually supplement their diet with a few insects to provide the protein and trace elements they require, and forsaking this natural diet for what is provided in the feeders means that they can become malnourished. This has been reported in Red Wattlebirds and Rainbow Lorikeets in the suburbs during winter – they've been found weakened, disoriented or just plain dead.

So while feeding birds can be a wonderful experience, if you don't want to turn your once healthy garden birds into lethargic, grumpy individuals who take over the couch and leave grubby claw prints over the remote and keep telling you every minute how bored they are, then approach feeding them very cautiously.

ACTION: If you really would like to attract birds to your garden then the best thing to do is to grow indigenous plants. They will create food and shelter for a wider range of birds instead of simply providing an easy meal for a select few. A birdbath placed strategically out of the reach of cats and other predators can also bring in the birds, though it too should be regularly cleaned to prevent the spread of disease.

Field guides / books that are an essential aid to bird identification.

The best time to use a field guide is before you have even set foot outside the door. Thoroughly perusing the pages of a good field guide is excellent preparation for knowing what to expect when you actually get out in the field. You may not remember every detail, but it is amazing how much will pop back into your mind when you are looking at a bird that you would normally have no idea about.

The serious birder would never be seen dead using a field guide in the field – they like to convey the impression that they know it all already. Personally, I am not averse to taking one along with me, because even after almost 30 years of birding I still get stumped occasionally. And it is amazing how quickly the experts will gather around when you pull one out of your backpack after you have seen an odd-looking bird.

The key is to not become a slave to your field guide. Even the best contain a few mistakes, and wild birds will occasionally not conform to how the field guides tell us they should look. But for some people, the field guide is gospel and a bird doesn't exist unless the good book has told them so.

On an expedition to the Torres Strait islands with some of Australia's leading twitchers, we managed to find a Papuan Flowerpecker, a New Guinea species that until recently wasn't even in any Australian field guide. Most of us had boned up on what we needed to look for and as soon as we had our binoculars trained on the bird we started yelling out each of the key features we could see – scarlet cap, throat and chest, red Undertail-coverts – until we were all satisfied we had definitely seen this rarity, whereupon we were all pumping the air in triumph, high-fiving; the usual sort of nonsense when you've all just seen a new bird.

But one guy had been quiet the whole time. He pulled the New Guinea field guide out of his rucksack, went to the appropriate page and began reading out all the diagnostic features, the very same ones we had been describing only moments before. Only after he had read every detail in full did he dramatically snap the book shut and declare, 'Congratulations, gentlemen, I do believe we have just seen a Papuan Flowerpecker!' Clearly for him, the word of four experienced birders was nothing unless confirmed in the field guide.

Another problem arises when the birder places undue emphasis on a particular diagnostic feature when a whole range of features in combination need to be taken into consideration. There has only been one accepted record of a Laysan Albatross in Australian waters, a bird found exhausted on Norfolk Island. Before it was released it was photographed, and all agreed that it was a classic Laysan; there could be no doubt. All except the birder who had put a ring on the bird. He had used a certain sized band on the bird, but on later consultation, discovered that a typical Laysan should take a different sized ring. In spite of all the countervailing evidence, he concluded that it must not in fact be a Laysan at all. He couldn't accept the possibility that the manual might have been wrong or that there could be an individual variation or simply that this bird had fat ankles.

And this phenomenon doesn't just occur in difficult-to-identify birds such as seabirds. In one edition of a field guide there was a printer's error which saw a red dot appear on the undertail of a Horsfield's Bronze-cuckoo, a bird that does not have any red in it. Suddenly people were reporting that they had seen a Horsfield's Bronze-cuckoo on the basis of the diagnostic red spot on the Undertail-coverts – an argument, if ever there was one, for taking a full set of notes before referring to the field guide, because it is far too easy to conflate what you actually saw in real life with what you saw on the page. After all, if you are looking at a field guide at the time you are looking at the bird, it takes a very disciplined memory to distinguish between the two later.

So which field guide is the best? I am going to cop out here and say that ultimately it is a personal choice. There are four that all are good in their own way, and if you are really serious, it is probably best to have all of them so that you can compare and contrast. The four are (in order of original publication), Simpson and Day, Slater, Pizzey and Knight, and Morecombe.

A 2003 survey of 165 subscribers to the Birding-aus website rated the preferred field guides in the following order: Pizzey and Knight (39% of respondents), Slater (30%), Simpson and Day (21%) and Morecombe (10%). I won't divulge how I would rank each of them, but a quick précis follows.

Simpson and Day is the guide I have used most; it has been the default field guide for me over the years, so much so that I rarely actually refer to it now, and often reach for the others so I can get a fresh perspective. There are many who dislike the layout of Simpson and Day and I must say that the design of the later editions does seem to be getting rather cluttered.

Many people opt for Slater because it is the smallest and therefore easiest to take into the field. Wimps. The main drawbacks of Slater are that it has a rather cursory text, and includes a few birds that aren't on the official list yet. While some of these are undoubtedly genuine, they haven't for whatever reason (*see* RARITIES COMMITTEE) been put to any rigorous verification. As outlined above with the Horsfield's Bronze red-spot special, once a bird is illustrated, people start miraculously reporting them (*see* HARRIERS).

The text in the Pizzey guide is probably the most comprehensive (and even better in its original incarnation, the house-brick-sized Pizzey and Doyle of 1980) and I find the illustrations in this book the most aesthetically pleasing, though it has to be said that at times Simpson and Day is far more accurate, particularly when it comes to the shape of birds.

The most recent arrival is Morecombe, which has a new format that is far more helpful to the beginner with many innovative features in its layout. It is particularly good for the different races of a species. I am not a great fan of the illustrations, especially when it comes to waders and seabirds, which are what I most often open a field guide to look at because they can be so damned tricky to identify. In fact if you really want to get a handle on those two groups of birds it would be best to obtain one of the international guides that focuses solely on them (which leads to a whole new kettle of kingfishers, fortunately beyond the scope of this book).

The best field guide of all, with almost every detail you would want on any bird would have to be *HANZAB* (*see* *HANZAB*). The only drawbacks are that it costs the equivalent of a year's wages (for this author anyway) and it is a handbook and not a field guide – you would need the shoulders of an East German swimmer or a small team of Sherpas to take all seven volumes into the field with you.

ACTION: Momentarily impress (and then bore the pants off) your friends at social gatherings by throwing them a field guide and getting them to read out the text randomly while you guess what bird they are talking about. Then again, if you are a hard-core birder you probably don't get invited to many functions any more.

Field guides, how to use them / if you don't know which bird you're looking for, how can you look it up? A nightmare for the novice birdwatcher.

One of the first things that novice birdwatchers confront when they begin birding is that the field guides are bloody confusing. Here are a few pointers on how to make sense of them.

Say you see a bird you haven't seen before. Not only have you no idea of what species it is, you are stumped as to even what family of birds it belongs to. You open the field guide and are confronted by a seemingly random selection of birds. The bird you have seen is a smallish, brownish bird. There is no section on smallish, brownish birds. They are not even presented alphabetically, so how the hell do you go about identifying it?

Unfortunately for the beginner, there is no getting around the fact that you will have to flick through page after page looking for a bird that approximates the one you saw. Some of the newer field guides have included an allegedly easy-find section, but this usually runs to just a page or two. Some regional guides such as Lloyd Nielsen's *Birds of Queensland's Wet Tropics and Great Barrier Reef* do have a section where you can compare birds of similar features (for example, black birds), but to do this with an Australia-wide field guide would be far too cumbersome as you tried to cross-reference all the different categories of birds. (The section on smallish, brownish birds could end up being another book in itself.)

If you saw your bird in the garden, perhaps the field guide might classify the birds by habitat. But it doesn't. One of the first field guides, Neville Cayley's *What Bird is That?* tried this many years ago but it became confusing because some birds range over many different habitats, and some turn up where they aren't supposed to be. All around the country you will get birds using different habitats. In Eastern Australia the Hooded Plover is found exclusively on sandy ocean beaches, whereas in Western Australia it gathers in flocks on inland salt lakes. To put it in one habitat category would be misleading; to slot it and every other bird into all applicable habitat headings would make the field guide so big you couldn't get it out the door.

It looks like you are stuck with the field guides in their current form. Like most things, they do get easier with familiarity. The first thing to know is that there is a method to the seeming random order of birds, and that is that they are grouped taxonomically, with the most ancient of families first. This is why you get birds such as Emus and ducks and penguins up near the start as it is believed these have been around the longest.

Basically the taxonomic order divides birds into two types, the passerines and the non-passerines. Generally speaking, the passerines are the songbirds – robins, wrens, thrushes – but a bird doesn't have to sing to be a passerine. The word 'passerine' actually refers to their feet; it essentially means 'perching bird'. It just so happens that most of the perching birds, conveniently, also sing. Generally, non-passerines don't sing, but they are more likely to screech, grunt, croak or coo. Everything that isn't a passerine is lumped into this category. So anything that doesn't strike you as a little singing type is probably a non-passerine. Anything like seabirds, ducks, eagles, parrots and pigeons will be in the non-passerine half of the book, which is always at the front because it is thought that the non-passerines are older in evolutionary terms. All the many types of passerines will be in the latter half of the book.

So if your little brown bird seems to be a bit of a singer (or to go back to the perching bird theme, if it has relatively normal size legs with no webbed feet, giant claws or anything odd), it will probably be a passerine. Hence you head to the back section of the book. This will still involve flicking through many pages, and you may come up with half a dozen or more little brown birds that it could be.

Now you have to start looking at other things beside the illustrations. I always look at the maps before the text because they can eliminate quite a lot of contenders. If you saw the bird in Adelaide and there is a likely-looking bird that is found no nearer than Western Australia, I'd say there's a pretty good chance it is not that bird, no matter how much you would like it to be, even if the picture looks right. Vagrant birds do turn up, but probably not in your garden, so it is better to investigate all the local possibilities thoroughly before launching into any great flights of fancy.

There is nothing for it; you will have to go through the text. It is a good idea not to rely on the name for too much guidance. The Brown-backed Honeyeater, for instance, is only one of more than a dozen honeyeaters that could be said to have a brown back; and, while the Blue-winged Parrot does indeed have a blue wing, so do the very similar Orange-bellied, Rock and Elegant Parrots. You will need to delve a little deeper, I'm afraid.

Eventually, after all that, you finally decide it is a female Brown Songlark because of its general brownish colour and shortish bill. Congratulations, you have successfully negotiated your field guide to clinch your first ID. The only trouble is, it was an immature Starling, which you didn't bother looking up because the adults are shiny black and the field guide you were using didn't illustrate the young birds.

Firsts / not just the first time you see a species, but the first record of a particular bird for the country; ensuing records are known as a second, third, fourth and so on.

Note that only the most pedantic birders bother to refer to anything more than a tenth, though some Asbirders types can probably name the dates and locations of every one of the first 25 or more records of a species, a bit like those people who can recite pi to a thousand places.

Even the most ardent anti-twitcher would find it hard to deny that the first time you see a bird is a pretty thrilling moment. No future encounter will have the same kind of buzz. So you can imagine the amplification of excitement in finding a first that no one else in the entire nation has seen.

In the twenty-first century it is highly unlikely that you would find a bird completely new to science; a fungus maybe, or an ant – there are plenty of them itching for the privilege of being assigned a card in the great filing cabinet of human knowledge – but a totally new bird species is extremely unlikely.

It is still possible, however, that someone will discover a first for Australia. That is, a bird that may commonly occur in other countries, but until you clap eyes on it, nobody has ever seen one here. To see a first for Aus gives a cachet that virtually nothing else in birdwatching can. There are no prizes other than the awe and respect of lesser mortals (though I do know of at least one twitcher who makes up a little plaque for himself to commemorate every first he finds), but it is the dream of probably every twitcher, probably every birder.

In my Big Twitch year, I saw 703 birds, but they were all birds other people had already found. I had pretty much resigned myself to being satisfied with finding a first for my state – Bridled Tern, Patterson Lakes, 28 December, 1998, first recorded Victorian sighting – because I was no chance of ever finding a new bird for the entire country. Or so I thought.

After previous false starts, I finally found myself in a birding party on Ashmore Reef, an island territory closer to Indonesia than it is to Australia. Other members of the party had already discovered two new species for Australia, the Asian Brown Flycatcher and Lesser Coucal, so the chances that an unprecedented third newie might turn up were exceedingly unlikely.

As the heat of the tropical sun began to lose its intensity we all gathered to search yet again for the coucal, a strange, dishevelled-looking type of cuckoo. We had flushed it just once each morning from the only patch of thick grass on the island. It did a remarkable job of remaining hidden from the prying eyes of eight desperate twitchers, and we had just finished another cordon through the prickly vegetation without success.

As we rested and discussed our options, I noticed a movement in the foliage of a nearby Octopus Bush. About the only small birds we had seen on the island in such bushes were Arctic Warblers (about the tenth recorded occurrence in Australian territory – a tenth – and Yellow Wagtails, a regular though hardly common visitor to the far north – about the 442nd). Thinking it was one of these two, I almost ignored the movement but upon investigating I realised it was something different.

It turned out to be a Middendorff's Grasshopper Warbler, the first ever Australian record of this nondescript warbler with the Pythonesque name. And I was the first person ever to lay eyes on it in this country. Of course, if the others hadn't been there I doubt whether the identity of the skulking bird would ever have been satisfactorily resolved – my first reaction was that I had no idea what what the hell it was, I only knew it was different. It took us a lot of scrambling about on our bellies to even find the bird again, but we got good photographs and later that night on the boat as we pored over the field guides until we were satisfied with our identification, it was an absolutely tremendous feeling of satisfaction. Not only a lifer (*see* LIFER), but a first for Australia, and one that I had found! Who knows, I might even have a little plaque made up.

Of course two years down the track I still haven't written it up to put before the Rarities Committee. It's a bit like scoring a goal at the World Cup and not running around with your jumper over your head pretending to be an aeroplane. All achievement, no recognition. Also no scrutiny; so until I do submit the Middy's (for we are on familiar terms now, we write practically every other day) the record remains untested and officially unsubstantiated.

 ACTION: I really must write this record up properly and submit it to the rarities committee (*see* RARITIES COMMITTEE). Oh, by the way, this action is meant for me, not for you, reader.

Flush / the term used to describe a bird flying out from cover.

The term can be used thus: 'The King Quail flushed from the dense grass in front of Brad and Angelina'.

It can also describe the act of a birder engaged in trying to get the bird to fly: 'Angelina and Brad moved into the dense grass hoping to flush a King Quail'.

And finally it describes the look on the face of the birder once they have seen their quarry: 'After flushing the King Quail, Angelina noticed that Brad's face was flushed red with excitement'.

It is not to be confused with that other type of flush: 'As the customs officials approached Brad with their sniffer dogs, Angelina desperately tried to flush the pills down the toilet'.

Four-wheel drive / a mode of transport that is capable of off-road travel, guzzles an enormous amount of fossil fuel, costs a whole lot more to run than a conventional vehicle and in 99 per cent of cases never actually leaves the bitumen.

Birdwatchers are one of the few groups of city dwellers that can legitimately claim they need a 4WD. Or do they really?

While 4WDs undoubtedly get you into some very remote areas full of great birds, as far as I can ascertain there are only two species in Australia that you simply cannot see without the aid of a 4WD (or a helicopter): Black Grasswren and Princess Parrot. Even then, the Princess Parrot has been seen at least once in the last five years by the side of the Lasseter Highway, the main sealed road between Alice Springs and Uluru.

There is a suite of birds confined to the rainforests on Cape York that are virtually impossible to get to in the wet season without a four-wheel drive. The group includes Red-bellied Pitta and Black-winged Monarch, which are New Guinea migrants that are only around in the Wet. But as it is theoretically possible to get through in the Dry in a conventional 2WD vehicle, the rest of these birds would be considered gettable. Of course your conventional vehicle may never be the same again and curl up into the foetal position whenever you mention Red-cheeked Parrot or Northern Scrub-robin.

Similarly, there are a couple of desert specialties such as Grey and Eyrean Grasswrens that you can get to without a 4WD, but there is every likelihood you will do your car an awful lot of damage. I speak from experience. I once took my father's lovely Toyota Cressida up through western Queensland to Innamincka and back again in search of such birds. The result – I dipped on both and did $5000 worth of damage to the chassis of my father's beloved car. Thank goodness he had died the year before, otherwise the shock would have killed him!

So it is possible in most cases to see a species without needing to engage the hubs of the 4WD, but there are a lot of other places where having an off-road vehicle makes things a hell of a lot easier. One instance is the Crab Creek Road, which leads to the Broome Bird Observatory; while a little corrugated, it is, in all but the worst conditions, driveable in a normal car. But it is officially designated as a 4WD-only road, and the Broome Shire Council has been known to issue fines for breaching this rule.

 ACTION: If you are worried that your car will attract derision as a 'Toorak Tractor', remember never to wash the dust off after a birding trip, and to whack a big birding organisation sticker on the back. Even better, have a sticker made up with the phrase (or write with your finger on the dusty rear window), 'I saw 48 new birds in the Kimberley with this car; how many did you get driving to the gym this morning?'

If you are still worried about the environmental impact of owning a 4WD, why not simply hire one for your next major birding trip? Off-road vehicles cost more to hire, but even a two-week stint in one is probably cheaper than the annual running costs of a big 4WD.

Gear freaks / freaks that love their gear.

Have you ever wondered why lots of tough kids, cool kids, were really into cricket when you were young? Here's a game that involves not much action and standing around in a hot field for days on end, and yet it attracts some of the real legends of the schoolyard. I think the simple explanation is that though cricket may be a tedious and dreary sport, it is replete with all sorts of equipment. The kid that is into cricket can happily spend hours oiling his bat, shining his ball and adjusting his pads and box, and that's even before he sets foot on the pitch. There seems to be a genetic predisposition in men that manifests itself very early, towards any sort of apparatus – the gear freak gene.

So it is with birding. Men and women gravitate towards birding because they are enchanted with the natural world, fascinated by these magical winged creatures, or are just sad loners who don't get along with others and need a legitimate hobby to mask their anti-social tendencies. But there is a certain type of male birdwatcher who becomes just as obsessed with the gear and accoutrements associated with birding as with birding itself.

Though all you need to go birding is a pair of binoculars, a field guide and a notebook – and even then you really could do away with all of them and still observe birds quite happily – these days there's a plenitude of gear to become freaky about. Binoculars, telescopes, tripods, cameras (both still and video), GPS devices, MP3 players, dictaphones, sound-recording equipment, digital notebooks, pagers, personal organisers, birding software, spotlights, night-vision goggles, mist nets, remote sensor devices, tracking devices, batteries, chargers, microphones, parabolic reflectors, EPIRBS, headlamps, maps, speakers, mirrors and ladders for checking nests, camping and 4WD gear – there is an almost endless selection to choose from.

But don't expect any advice on gear from this book. I am a total Luddite when it comes to all this stuff and I would much rather be out in the bush actually looking at birds. You think getting into a conversation with a rabid birder is bad enough; try getting stuck in a corner at a party with a birder who is also into sonogram recording technology and digiscope photography and is developing a software package to identify bird species from the chemical composition of their droppings. Suicide never looked so good!

Girlfriends / to the rabid bird-nerd, as rare as a sighting of a Night Parrot.

Actually, that is a fairly cheap shot, and simply not true. Surprising as it might seem, the majority of younger birders, particularly the twitcher types, seem to have a girlfriend, and not the bookish nerdette that you might imagine. In my experience, in the vast majority of cases the girlfriend of a birder is a smart, sexy, independent-minded woman. What the hell is going on?

Maybe it is the seductive atmosphere of a bird hide, or the alluring way that those binoculars dangle around his neck, but there's another possible explanation. Believe it or not, many twitchers are quite charismatic. In order to survive the hell of being a high-school birdwatcher, they have surely developed a skin so thick, or have been so confident in themselves, that they have had no need to seek the approval of others. Hence you have birdwatcher as rebel; he plays by his own rules. This is, my female friends assure me, a very attractive quality.

If only I had cottoned on to this fact in all the years I was single.

Gonads (the duck's nuts) / one of the most brilliant yet scandalously underused naughty words in the language.

Now a lot of readers may think that this topic appears in these pages for totally puerile motives. And they'd most probably be right. But I kid you not; one of the most common questions I am asked once people know that I am a birdwatcher is, 'Do birds have a penis?'

I find it intriguing that so many are so desperate to know the status of a grackle's tackle. (I know a grackle is not an Australian bird, but it seemed a lot classier to mention than a rosella's fella, a hobby's knobby, or a treecreeper's peeper – yes, much classier.) And to save the reader from conducting their own Internet search which can trip all sorts of filters, not to mention sending you to many a website that would look very embarrassing on your search history, here is the answer to that burning question.

The simple response is that some birds do and some birds don't. Clearly, the females don't have a penis, but then again, in most species, neither do the males. In fact they both have what is called a cloaca, a type of cavity that contains both the reproductive and digestive tracts. The word comes from the Latin for sewer, which is a tad unromantic. It certainly puts a dampener on the idea of the quaintly named cloacal kiss which is the way most birds mate. The male stores his sperm in his cloaca and by touching the female's cloaca, he transfers them into the female where they greet the unfertilised eggs.

So rather than talking about a parrot's carrot or a currawong's schlong, one should more correctly refer to a shag's bag and a rook's nook. Although one of my favourite sayings, 'the duck's nuts', still holds true to an extent as ducks and other waterfowl, along with some others like Emu, actually do have penises of sorts. In fact, one species, the Argentine Lake Duck possesses a member that stretches to 42.5 cm, slightly longer than the duck itself!

It is interesting that most of those birds with penises are from very ancient families of birds. In most other animals, it is the more recent species that have developed penises (such as mammals). Perhaps it's an evolutionary thing: having an appendage dangling along in flight would not be the most aerodynamic of designs and so the cloaca made a triumphant re-emergence.

So there you have it, hopefully a definitive answer on what is clearly uppermost in many people's mind. And I promise that the schoolboy humour ends here …

Well, just a couple more: a snipe's pipe, a pitta's fritter and a whistler's gristler. There, it's out of my system now.

Grey Falcon / 1. a mythical bird that doesn't exist. 2. a car manufactured by Ford that is grey in colour.

Not that you would ever confuse 1 with 2 as the latter is a car and the former is a bird of prey of Central Australia that, despite looking at over a dozen sites the length and breadth of the land, I still haven't managed to see. This is probably because the bird doesn't exist in the first place, having been invented by an evil cabal of twitchers, wanting to play a joke on unsuspecting birders. Either that, or it was the Outback Chamber of Commerce who invented a bird so plausibly elusive that it would keep idiot twitchers with fat wallets returning to otherwise barren landscapes.

Grey Falcon sightings / sightings of the mythical Grey Falcon; in other words, lies, because Grey Falcons do not exist.

Any reported sightings come from one of three groups:

1. outright stringers (*see* STRINGERS)

2. members of the evil twitching cabal (*see* GREY FALCON)

3. people who have seen a regular Brown Falcon spray-painted grey by the evil cabal (*see* AN OPTOMETRIST AS CLEARLY YOU NEED YOUR EYES TESTED IF YOU ARE FOOLED BY THAT).

Grey-headed Lapwing / a type of wader (*see* WADER) that normally inhabits the marshes of Manchuria.

The lone Grey-headed Lapwing that somehow found its way to the small northern New South Wales town of Burren Junction in 2006 became the most famous and probably most looked-at bird in Australian birdwatching history. Perhaps the Red-necked Crake that appeared every evening at the pool by the orchard of the Kingfisher Park Birdwatchers' Lodge in north Queensland may have been seen by more people, but that has been over a period of 40-odd years, so chances are it wasn't actually the same bird.

More than 350 birders made the long trek to Burren Junction (the closest capital city was Sydney, a mere 600 kilometres away) which meant that not only did the local café owners make so many bacon-and-egg sandwiches to feed the hungry twitchers that they can now bring their retirement plans forward by a couple of years, but also that a new era in Australian twitching may have dawned.

It was as if the Grey-headed Lapwing represented a critical mass in Australia's twitching history. It wasn't just the rump of hard-core twitchers that went chasing it; many respectable birders joined in the fun. And fun they seemed to have as many shared for the first time in the joyful insanity of heading halfway across a continent to look for a single bird that may not be there when you get there.

That said, I don't think we are approaching the British situation, where thousands of twitchers will stake out a rarity in a field or supermarket carpark hoping for a glimpse. At least not yet. When only a couple of months later Australia's first twitchable Sabine's Gull turned up at Derby in the north-west of Western Australia, probably no more than a dozen birders went to see it. Not surprising when you consider that for most Aussie birdwatchers Derby is a full day's flight away, and perhaps everyone had already used up their twitching tickets on the lapwing. But it will be interesting to see what happens the next time a mega-rarity turns up within striking distance of a major city.

Gripped off / what happens to you when a birder who has seen a bird that you haven't been able to find reminds you of this fact with great glee.

As Bill Oddie observed, being gripped off is not nearly as pleasant as it sounds. In fact, for a birdwatcher, being gripped off is far worse than dipping (*see* DIP), as not only have you not seen the bird, but a rival has. Let's not pretend here – whatever twitchers may say about the competition only being against yourself, the truth is that twitching is a competitive sport. Being gripped off hurts even more if the person gripping you off is a bit of a duffer (*see* DUFFER). It's like the Australian cricket team being beaten by a cricketing minnow such as Bangladesh, Holland or England.

From the other side of the fence, things look very different. It's impossible not to get just a little bit of malicious glee out of another twitcher's suffering. That said, I only grip off close friends and even then I am quite selective (gee, that sentence would sound grubby in any other context). I have known some birders to go into a deep depressive malaise lasting a week if they suffer a major dip. In cases like this it is best to back off as they are doing a great job of gripping themselves off, if you know what I mean.

Here are a few effective gripping strategies:

1. Implying only a duffer could have missed it: 'Oh, didn't you see the Little Curlew? It was showing really well before.'

2. Putting in the patronising get-out clause, but still really saying that only a duffer could have missed it: 'Are you sure you were looking in the right place? You couldn't really miss the Northern Shoveller if you were at the right place.'

3. The outright bastard gloat: 'I can't believe you didn't see it, it was an absolute crippler! (*see* CRIPPLER) One of the best birding experiences of my life! I've seen some good birds in my time but that breeding-plumaged Spoon-billed Sandpiper was the most awesome bird ever!'

 ACTION: As soon as you have delivered your killer grip-off, run like crazy before other birders clock you with their telescope.

Guides, books / one way of increasing your chances of seeing a particular bird (or a whole range of birds) is to consult a 'where to find' birding guide.

One thing to remember with a guidebook is that things can change almost as soon as the book is printed. Birds do have a habit of flying away, so just because the author of a guidebook saw a Partridge Pigeon at such-and-such a place does not mean that you will. I find it incredible when birders slag off a guidebook on this basis, as if the authors are personally responsible for them dipping out. When an author writes that they saw a Carpentarian Grasswren 27.8 kilometres along a certain road and somebody dips at that site, it doesn't mean the author was stringing (*see* STRINGER); it might just be that the birds are in some almost identical habitat along the other 27.7 kilometres along that stretch. Until a guidebook to where all Australia's birds are nailed down is written, this problem will be inevitable.

I have, however, had one experience where the guidebook was spookily accurate. While looking for Grey Honeyeater, an extremely scarce bird whose range stretches across vast areas of desert without it being common anywhere, I had a copy of Richard and Sarah Thomas's *The Complete Guide to Finding the Birds of Australia* (known as Thomas and Thomas) open on the passenger's seat next to me. I knew that the birds had been seen at the site mentioned in Thomas and Thomas very recently, and was mainly using the book to orient myself. To get my bearings, I drove to the exact spot mentioned in the book. I pulled up at the precise spot, and as I turned off the engine a pair of Grey Honeyeaters flew into the nearest tree! Nothing like that has ever happened to me since.

 ACTION: If you are after a good guidebook, there have been a few attempts at devising a 'where to find' guide for Australia. The first by John Bransbury was not too bad but a little eclectic in the locations he had chosen. Despite relying on information fifteen years old, the Thomas and Thomas book is still of great value. But the most up-to-date guide is one self-published by Lloyd Nielsen, a highly respected north Queensland birder. Updated every year, Lloyd's book has both an international and Australian edition to cater for the different needs of the local and overseas birder. There are also some very good local guides, such as McCrie and Watson's guide, *Finding Birds in Darwin, Kakadu and the Top End* and Jo Wieneke's *Where to Find Birds in North-east Queensland*.

Guides, personal / a birder with local knowledge employed by other birders to help them find target species.

To the purists who pride themselves on their ability to hunt a species out for themselves, the thought of hiring a guide is anathema, the equivalent of paying for sex. But really all it is doing is formalising and setting a price for a process that goes on all the time in birding: the exchange of information. (Hmm, maybe it does sound little bit like paying for sex!) I think some turn their nose up at guides because they think it's a tacit admission that they don't have the requisite knowledge or the connections to find a bird for themselves. In a subculture where, until recently, knowledge was shared among relatively few people, there was a pride in being part of the loop. Bird guides in any form open up these opportunities to the great unwashed. I can understand where such prejudice comes from, but let's face it, it is terribly elitist. And besides, bird guiding is a profession that allows a lot of great birders the opportunity to make a living out of their passion.

Having said that, I have never paid for a guide myself (Do I sound like a politician? 'I did not go birding with that woman!'), but I have been fortunate on a number of occasions when I have been in an unfamiliar area to have been shown around by a knowledgeable local, which made it a hell of a lot easier to get good value out of the trip.

There is a whole range of issues involved when hiring a guide, and surprisingly, their ability to find birds is not necessarily the most important. I know one guide who led a couple of tours of American birders around Australia and he said the only time he ever had any real trouble was when it came to catering arrangements. One group almost mutinied over the issue of beetroot – the Yanks aren't so keen on the old beetroot in their sandwiches and apparently every sandwich-maker across Australia insists on using beetroot. It didn't matter that the group had just seen over 400 species of bird, including some highly sought-after ones like the Yellow Chat and Gouldian Finch; the fact that their sangers were a soggy purple almost ruined the trip for them.

Most professional guides are used to all sorts of clients, so they should be able to tailor their services to your needs. There are a few types of guide to avoid, however.

1. The rabid twitcher

This is the type of birding guide that is using your dollar to get as many birds on their own list as they can. This can be great if you have a similar aim, but sometimes you will be wanting to see a particular bird, not everything that is gettable within a 200-kilometre range. On the other side of the fence, I know of many birding guides who sacrificed potential lifers because they have had to attend to their clients' needs first. It must be agonising knowing you have to turn your back on your possible first-ever Oriental Reed-warbler in order to show a visitor a Magpie Goose for the nine-hundredth time.

2. The duffer

Even at the best of times, duffers are to be avoided, but when you are lumbered with one as a guide it can turn what should have been a great trip into an utter disaster. Generally a duffer won't last too long in the industry, as word will get around, but if the tour is organised privately you may accept what seems to be the kindly invitation of a local to take you around an area you are visiting, only to find that you are trapped in a car with someone who sees you as fresh meat for their repertoire of interminable go-nowhere stories, crackpot theories and dodgy birdwatching skills.

3. The wildlife tour guide

Some places such as resorts or larger national parks have what are usually called 'wildlife tours'. No matter what the advertising material might say, it is unlikely that these tour guides will be tailoring their trips for birders. After all, your average tourists might be interested momentarily in seeing pelicans or emus or sea eagles and other large, prominent birds, but their attention will quickly be drawn back to the non-birding highlights such as crocodiles. Man, do tourists love crocodiles.

What is particularly galling is when these types of tours are the only way a birder can access certain sites. Often the guides may know a bit about conspicuous birds such as kingfishers or herons, but chances are they will be stumped when it comes to the intricacies of identifying the masses of small waders feeding out on nearby mudflats, and they are hardly likely to stop the party to wait while you check out that female fairy-wren that you saw disappear into the bushes.

 ACTION: If you really need a little extra time to nail that fairy-wren ID, just point and yell, 'Crocodile!' The tour will stop for at least five minutes trying to find it. This will work anywhere, though on a desert tour it may succeed just the once before they get suspicious.

Gun / 1. before good optical equipment became generally available, the gun was the primary tool used by birders to identify birds. 2. a hot-shot birder.

A gun birder isn't necessarily the one with the greatest list, though if they wanted to it probably wouldn't take them long to accumulate a grand total. A gun is the infuriating type who manages to nail the identification of that Arctic Warbler before you have even registered there is even a bird in the vicinity. A gun is the annoying guy who always seems to be in the right place for that perfect photograph of the Kerguelen Petrel as it flashes past the boat in its one and only fly-by of the day, or if you spread out looking for the Red-chested Button-quail this is the character who will have one flush at his feet. It is not luck (*see* JAMMY PETE), it is skill.

I am full of admiration for gun birders but I secretly resent them because, until they turn up, dude birdwatchers believe I am a gun.

Habitat / the specific environment in which a bird lives.

Preservation of habitat is the single most important issue in bird conservation. Some birds can adapt to several habitats or exploit a niche in a new habitat as it opens up. Others are specialists and can only survive in one particular habitat. But the bottom line is that all birds need a habitat of some sort: somewhere that provides the three basics of life: food, shelter and Internet access. Or in the case of a bird, a mate.

The more you go birdwatching, the more you actually end up going habitat-hunting. After a while you get to know the habitat requirements of each species and realise that there is no point looking for a Mangrove Golden Whistler too far from mangroves or a Spinifexbird in an area where there is no spinifex. Not that you can set too much store by the manner in which birds are named, for while a Grass Owl is usually to be found in swamp-like grassy areas, hardly any of the grasswrens are to be found in habitat you would conceivably call 'grassy'. Similarly, field-wrens are far more likely to be found in scrub than fields, Olive Whistlers are never found in olive trees, and I have yet to see a Fairy Penguin lining up in the Sydney Mardi Gras.

With experience you can develop a feel for the habitat preference of many a species of bird. On countless occasions

I have been with birders and one of us has said, 'This looks like a good spot for a Speckled Warbler, or Spotless Crake, or Chestnut-breasted Quail-thrush, and seconds later, sure enough, a warbler or a crake or a quail-thrush has popped up directly in front of us.

Actually, I am lying about the quail-thrush. In 2002 I spent days trekking through likely habitat, saying, 'I reckon this looks good for a Chestnut-breasted Quail-thrush', only to be disappointed time after time. Every time I am birding at my local patch, Seaford Swamp, I always intone, 'There's got to be a Painted Snipe here!' as if I could will one into being. So far it hasn't worked.

 ACTION: Next time you are out birding, make a note of the location, but also the kind of habitat you have seen a particular bird in: note type and size of dominant tree, density of undergrowth, how close to water, that sort of thing. And if you see that same species again somewhere else, compare the areas you saw it in. Pretty soon you will build a mental image of what type of habitat a bird prefers. It will help you find the bird again, and can even help you decide where to look, or where not to look for a similar type of bird in a different area.

HANZAB / *The Handbook of Australian, New Zealand and Antarctic Birds*, published in seven volumes by Birds Australia.

HANZAB was a significant milestone in Australasian natural history. How big? For the birdwatching community, the completion of *HANZAB* is every bit as big as Ron Barassi's injunction to his players at half-time in the 1970 Grand Final to 'Handball, handball, handball!' is to AFL football.

It all began back in the 1970s when three members of the then RAOU (now Birds Australia) board, discussed the idea of compiling a handbook of everything that was known about all of Australia's birds. Two of the three would not live to see the project through to fruition – it was finally completed in 2006 and stretched from an intended four volumes to seven, each the size of the Shanghai phonebook. It took Birds Australia more than twenty years and millions of dollars to see the project finalised.

The volumes were released a year or two apart, as quickly as the funds could be raised to pay the team of editors and researchers to compile the next one. In the lead-up to each volume's publication, the birding community would be like a kid at Christmas, waiting with bated breath for the presents to arrive. Sometimes Christmas was postponed a year or two and the wait was a lot longer than anticipated, but every time it was more than worth it, and birders would spend hours poring over each new volume – among them the small but dedicated band who would race to be the first to find a typo or layout error or incorrect fact amongst the thousands of pages. I can just imagine these self-styled experts sitting there, like the Comic Book Guy from *The Simpsons*, in the comfort of their own loungerooms, poring over every page in the race to be the first to proclaim, 'worst *HANZAB* ever!'

HANZAB is a truly massive work: it catalogues the 957 species of birds in the region, their plumage, range, habitats, even songs. The sheer volume, scope and depth on display in over 9000 information-crammed pages is staggering to behold. It has loads of the sort of information that will have your average bird aficionado engaged in bed-time reading for years (where else would you find in the one text a description of the adult post-breeding moult of a Chestnut-breasted Mannikin and eleven pages devoted to the food preferences of the Silvereye?).

HANZAB synthesised everything that had been published about our birds at the time (and then some; the *HANZAB* editors ended up having to do their own scientific research, particularly in the area of identification and plumages, because there were simply so many gaps in our knowledge). No field guide comes close in accuracy, detail or depth of information. Whenever I come across a strange bird in the field I will turn to my field guides first, but will always ultimately end up at *HANZAB* when I want definitive answers.

Often *HANZAB* isn't capable of supplying those answers, for despite all its vast accumulated knowledge, there are still enormous gaps in what we know about our birds. And as birds are one of the most obvious of creatures in our environment, imagine what we don't know about mammals, fish, fungi, insects and pretty much everything else we share this part of the world with.

 ACTION: If you can possibly afford it (it costs the equivalent of two twitching trips to Christmas Island), a complete set of *HANZAB* is a brilliant investment. One day they may publish an online version where you can extract the sections you want, but as the entire editing team and staff of Birds Australia are financially, emotionally and physically exhausted after finishing the last volume, I wouldn't hold your breath.

Harriers / not only have they lent their name to a very cool fighter plane, harriers are a type of bird of prey that are very cool in their own right.

In Australia we have two species, though most field guides give the impression that we have three. The reason for this is that along with the resident Swamp and Spotted Harriers, most illustrate the Papuan Harrier as well, based on the many unconfirmed reports of this bird, mainly from north Queensland and the Northern Territory.

The trouble is, they are all *unconfirmed*; there has not as yet been a single verified sighting (*see* VERIFICATION). But because they are illustrated in the books, people keep thinking they see them. What is not depicted in any of the books – even *HANZAB*, though it does mention it in the text – is the rare plumage phase of Swamp Harrier that can make it look a lot like a Papuan Harrier.

Travelling through north Queensland's Atherton Tableland (site of quite a few Papuan Harrier claims), I came across a harrier that I was convinced had to be a Papuan. It certainly was unlike any I harrier I had seen before. I knew from *HANZAB* that there was a post-juvenile hooded phase of Spotted Harrier, but this bird had a pale head. Luckily it hung around for half an hour and I got some reasonable photos and video footage of the bird. The natural pessimist in me had taken hold and I had pretty much talked myself out of it being the rarer one, a conclusion confirmed when I showed the photos to some experts who identified it as an immature female Spotted Harrier – admittedly, the palest they had ever seen.

If I hadn't already been alert to the variability of our common harriers, I would have turned to the field guides and even though the bird didn't quite fit, I would have probably hammered it into the Papuan Harrier slot in my checklist.

So I don't have Papuan Harrier on my list, but for that brief time I knew the thrill of seeing something potentially very exciting; the simultaneous feeling of exhilaration and wanting to poop my pants out of fear that nobody would ever believe me.

Hide / what birds usually do when I am looking for them; also a structure used to shield observers so the birds are not disturbed by the presence of humans.

Usually it is a man-made structure (and usually positioned by the authorities in the place most unlikely to have any actual birds in front of it, and with the sun right in your eyes) but the astute birder can use natural features such as trees or banks to screen themselves from the birds for as long as possible (*see* STALKING).

Hot spots / those areas in a forest or wetland or where two habitat zones merge, where there just seem to be more birds around than anywhere else.

You can be walking through the bush, not seeing a thing, when bang: suddenly the air is full of song and you are in the middle of a midday bird rave. The same principle applies on a broader scale – there are some areas that are just simply better for birds than others.

Of course, as usual it comes down to habitat quality and diversity. There are hundreds of such places all around the country, so to narrow it down to just a few hot spots does a great many wonderful birding sites a huge disservice. But as we all love a good list (come on, admit it, you love one just as much as me) I'll give you a list of my top ten birding hot spots around the country.

The criteria for inclusion are:

- The area must have a good range and diversity of birds. While the Nullarbor Plain may be a great site for the Rufous Fieldwren and Inland Dotterel, and the only location to get the Nullarbor race of the Cinnamon Quail-thrush, the truth is that you are hardly likely to see another bird out there.

- The said birds must be generally in evidence on a typical visit. There is nothing more disheartening than turning up to a site with a great bird list only to find it is as dead as the Nullarbor Plain in anything but an exceptionally good season.

- The quality of the birds that are present (for example, a cluster of endangered or endemic species) might push a place ahead of an area with a far greater birdlist.

- Finally, there is that intangible quality that goes beyond the actual birds themselves: the scenery, the remoteness, the general feeling of wellbeing that comes over you when you are in a spectacular natural environment. Sure, you might not find a Night Parrot or a Buff-breasted Sandpiper there, but when you are at these places you probably don't care.

So here it is, possibly the one reason why some birders have bothered to pick this book up. They have waded through the inconsequential drivel about ethics and girlfriends and parents and ducks' gonads and headed straight to this section in the hope of picking up some good places in which to chase ticks. They will probably be disappointed because there are no real secrets in my list of top ten birding hot spots. Here they are, not necessarily in any particular order.

Iron Range, Far North Queensland

Iron Range is a simply stunning area. Australia's largest lowland rainforest, it's the one place in Australia where you really feel you are in the jungle. It is simply teeming with life; not only many of the twenty or so birds you don't find anywhere else in Australia outside Cape York, but more mammals, reptiles and insects than I have ever seen in one place.

Broome, Western Australia

You could include the entire Kimberley as a hot spot, but as it is the size of Victoria, it qualifies as more of a hot region. Broome has a surprising array of bush birds inhabiting what at first might seem rather lifeless pindan plains. But Broome really stands out for the sheer exuberance of waterbirds, in particular waders. Roebuck and Eighty Mile Bays together provide one of the most crucial sites on the planet for migratory shorebirds, with tens and tens of thousands gathering to feed on the rich life of the mudflats. The numbers and diversity are mind-boggling, and to make it even sweeter, Broome turns up probably more vagrants than any other part of the mainland.

Lamington National Park, Queensland

Named after the same Queensland Governor who inspired the archetypal Aussie cake, Lamington National Park is simply one of the most beautiful places to go birdwatching. As you drive up the narrow, winding mountain roads to one of its two access points, the habitat changes from grasslands to woodland to subtropical forest until you find yourself on top of the plateau in temperate rainforest, including the mystical and ancient Antarctic Beech forests. The rainforest at Lamington is probably the loveliest forest I have ever been in, and as an added bonus, contains some highly sought-after species such as Albert's Lyrebird and Rufous Scrub-bird.

Capertee Valley, New South Wales

I could have mentioned Chiltern in Victoria as my favourite woodland birding site in the country, but Capertee just pips it because it has a slightly bigger bird list and a far greater likelihood of an appearance from its star attraction, the

Regent Honeyeater. About 200 kilometres from Sydney, this valley is the last stronghold of this once-common species. Add to the mix some impressive scenery and a whole swag of sought-after birds like Plum-headed Finch, Turquoise Parrot and Rock Warbler, and you've got yourself a hot spot, partner.

Kakadu National Park, Northern Territory

With everything from spinifex-clad sandstone escarpments to vast floodplains that attract hundreds of thousands of waterbirds, Kakadu has got the lot on the birding front. On top of all of this is the magic about the place itself; the vast scale of the landscape and a cultural heritage that goes back beyond 20 000 years, all combining to make Kakadu an unforgettable birding experience.

Cairns, Queensland

Without doubt, this is Australia's premier birdwatching area, with well over 380 species being recorded, more than anywhere else in Australia. Even though the city itself is a bit tawdry and over-developed, within an hour of Cairns are coral reefs, mangroves, mudflats, rivers, swamps, grasslands, tropical woodland, lowland and upland rainforest, all of which support a large suite of bird species. And as the weather is invariably warm at all times of the year, it is impossible for birders not to spend their entire visit to the Cairns region without huge smiles plastered across their faces.

Gluepot Reserve, South Australia

Strange name, brilliant birding. There are many great mallee reserves that provide excellent birding – Hattah-Kulkyne, Wyperfeld and Round Hill to name three – but Gluepot, a reserve owned and managed by Birds Australia, is hard to beat. Lying just north of South Australia's Riverland, it retains some of the best quality old-growth mallee habitat in the country, with a corresponding crop of quality mallee birds, including Black-eared Miner, Red-lored Whistler and Scarlet-chested Parrot.

Christmas Island

In terms of spectacular scenery and numbers of nesting seabirds, Lord Howe Island would probably just pip Christmas Island. Where this tropical island has the edge is in its land birds. It not only has six endemic breeding land birds, but its proximity to Indonesia means that many overshooting Asian migrants end up there. Christmas Island alone would have contributed half of the new birds for the Australian list in the last twenty years. And if enough birders keep birding there, it will probably propel the Australian list close to the 900 mark within another twenty years.

Two Peoples Bay, Western Australia

This rather small reserve near Albany (which in itself is a top birding location) certainly punches above its weight. In particular, it is famous as the site of the rediscovery of the Noisy Scrub-bird, which was believed extinct for 70 years. Also present in this spectacular location are other highly elusive species such as Western Bristlebird and Western Whipbird.

Bruny Island, Tasmania

This picturesque island not too far from Hobart boasts not only wonderful coastal and mountain views, but contains all twelve of Tasmania's endemics, including one of the biggest populations of the Forty-spotted Pardalote.

Of course, there are a myriad other areas which could quite rightly feel miffed at not making this list: Werribee, Kununurra, Darwin, Cunnamulla, the Hunter Valley and many more. And I haven't even mentioned Seaford Swamp, my local patch. But I had to cut the list off somewhere.

Identification / the origin of more contention in the birdwatching world than any other topic; even bigger than taxonomy and whether birds have penises (*see* TAXONOMY, GONADS).

A newcomer to birding might be on a bit of a roll. They have managed to identify those parrots that come and feed in the almond tree as Eastern Rosellas, and have been able to work out that the black-and-white bird that they have seen swimming at the pond in the local park is not actually a duck but a Little Pied Cormorant. But then a small bird arrives in the back yard that has them stumped. The novice birder looks at the multitude of pictures staring up from the page of a field guide, throws the book away and decides to take up a less frustrating pastime like finding needles in haystacks.

It needn't be like that. The processes that the top birdwatcher uses in identifying birds are those that we all use every day. If I was to show most Australians a picture of the West Coast Eagles, they would instantly be able to name what team it was, or at the very least, what sport they played.

So what happens when somebody looks at a picture of the West Coast Eagles? First, they see that they are members of a football team, because of the uniform and perhaps the presence of a football. And the style of uniforms themselves would establish that these are AFL and not Rugby League players. That and the fact that they have necks.

Looking more closely at a West Coast footballer, the observer would note the blue and yellow colours. More subtle indications of identification could be the time of year of the sighting – if an AFL player was seen on the last Saturday of September, it is a fair chance, in recent years, that he is likely to be a West Coast Eagle; small accoutrements, such as a premiership medallion dangling around the neck; or distinctive behaviours, such as getting into a drunken fight outside a casino at four in the morning or running away from a police booze bus.

All these indicators are processed within the blink of an eye because we have had years of reinforcement in learning them. The same thing applies when you're looking at birds – the more you look, the easier it will become. But how to get started?

Let's say you see a bird in your back yard in Bendigo that you think might be a honeyeater. You open a field guide to the honeyeater section. To your horror, there are around 67 to choose from. Don't let the abundance of choices overwhelm you. Even though Bendigo is one of the best regions in the country for honeyeaters, no single area is ever going to have many more than 25 genuine candidates. It always pays to check where a bird is supposed to be, for while the odd bird can and does turn up almost anywhere, most of them don't. And despite our overactive imaginations and desire for the exotic, you always eliminate the most likely before you even think about moving on to the unlikely.

But even 25 is still a daunting number of possibilities. And each of those will possess a head-spinning number of individual characteristics that combine to define what species they are. The trick is not to try and learn them all at once, but to focus on a few key features.

General colour is a handy one. Like the blue and yellow of the West Coast uniform, a predominantly black-and-white colour scheme might suggest a New Holland, Painted or even Regent Honeyeater; similarly if your bird is greenish in colour, you immediately rule the former three species out and narrow the possibilities down considerably.

Size is also a good one – just as you can tell a ruckman from a rover by how big they are, so you can separate a wattlebird from a spinebill. And then you can move on to other obvious traits like the size and shape of the bill. A spinebill, for instance, has a long, thin, down-curved bill that often has people mistakenly calling them hummingbirds. The Noisy Friarbird has something of a down-curved bill too, but you will soon realise that it is nothing like as delicate as the much smaller spinebill, and the friarbird has a ruddy great bald black noggin to boot.

This could still leave you with a suite of mid-sized honeyeaters that to the untrained eye still all look the same. This is where 'the standard unit' comes into play. All it requires is that you are able to manage to identify one species of bird initially, and then you begin to work out what the differences are between your mystery bird and your standard unit.

So if you have been able to nut out that the regular honeyeater in your yard is the White-naped Honeyeater, then try to work out how the bird you are now looking at is different. Perhaps this bird is more greyish than the green-backed tinge of a White-naped Honeyeater; perhaps it doesn't have the black head or red crescent over the eye. Noticing these differences enables you to work out what the bird isn't, which eventually will lead you to what it actually is (in this case, you believe it's a Fuscous Honeyeater).

Except in this case, you are wrong. It's actually a White-throated Treecreeper. Your initial assumption that it was a honeyeater was incorrect.

You get the point though, don't you? This is actually the process I use all the time when I'm out birdwatching, particularly when it comes to difficult groups of birds such as the waders.

If you consider the honeyeaters a difficult group to work out, you ain't seen nothin' yet. There have been around 77 wader species recorded in Australia, a significant minority of which are very infrequent visitors (*see* WADER). Add to this the fact that there are another 140 species in the world, of which twenty or so are migratory species that could feasibly turn up in Australia. Especially in non-breeding plumage, they can look very similar to each other. So much so that I have heard some very good birders declare that they don't even bother when it comes to waders because they are too hard.

To aid me in wader identification, I adopt the standard unit method, using the Sharp-tailed Sandpiper. The Sharpie is chosen partly because it is about the most common migratory wader that I regularly see, and because in many ways it is the prototype wader – it is about mid-size (or at least one of the larger of the small waders), its bill, though small, is not as short as some, and the same is true of its legs. I have become so familiar with Sharp-tailed Sandpipers that a quick scan through a flock of waders will give me an idea if there is anything different. Anything smaller and it is likely to be a stint, anything larger and you start to think about godwits, shanks and curlews. Anything that is grey, as opposed to the Sharpie's brownish plumage, immediately puts you in mind of a Curlew Sandpiper or Greenshank, or maybe a tattler. Anything with a longer bill than the Sharpie could be a Terek Sandpiper or godwit if the bill is upturned, a Curlew Sandpiper or curlew if it's downturned. Always referring back to the prototype lets you know where you are in the messy world of wader ID.

ACTION: This standard unit technique can also be applied to people. Just pick a prototype face and compare everyone you meet to it. 'Louise was like Nicole but her hair wasn't red.' 'Fred was like Brad but his eyes were brown, and he was a woman.' 'Margaret was like Angelina except she didn't have dark hair and she didn't make me feel all funny inside.' You'll never get a name wrong again.

Injured bird / something you should never take to a birdwatcher; they will identify it, make note of any anomalies in plumage, but when it comes to actually helping the bird they will be generally useless.

I am often presented with or phoned up about sick or injured birds that somebody has found. What am I meant to do with them? I don't have a degree in Veterinary Science. All I know is keep the bird overnight in a warm, dry place with access to some water. Nine out of ten times when you check on it the next morning it will either be dead or sufficiently recovered to be champing at the bit to get out of its box or cage. Many birds are injured by striking windows; they seem to be on their last wings when all they actually are is dazed and concussed, and they will miraculously do a Lazarus job given enough time.

The only other thing you can do with an injured bird, particularly if it has physical damage like a broken wing, is to take it to your local vet or wildlife shelter or network, such as WIRES or one of those groups. But don't be surprised or too upset if they euthanase the bird, because there is often little else that can be done.

ACTION: The chances of a bird with a type of bird flu that can be transmitted to humans turning up in Australia are infinitesimal, but just to be on the safe side (and there are other avian diseases as well) you shouldn't pick up any sick, injured or dead birds unless you are wearing protection, such as rubber gloves, and you should wash your hands thoroughly immediately after handling.

Internet / the biggest change to the way we bird-watch since binoculars were invented.

Photographs, trip reports, maps, equipment advice and purchase, newsgroups, discussion forums and (most crucially), information on where birds are turning up are now just a few keystrokes away. Bird-nerds, being the obsessive types they are, have taken to the Internet with a vengeance. Big Twitch Institute research has shown that when it comes to frequency of Internet use, birdwatchers are third only to sad, lonely guys downloading Russian porn, and fourteen-year-old girls checking out their MySpace sites to see how many friends they have.

Twitching in particular has changed forever with the advent of the Internet. Until recently, twitchers belonged to a fairly exclusive club. If you weren't in the loop, then the first you would hear about a rare bird turning up was when the sighting was written up in a scientific paper or when it made an appearance in the next edition of your field guide – usually several years after the bird had flown. Conversely, if a birder wasn't in the loop (or more accurately, one of many small loops) and saw a rarity, chances are no twitcher would ever get to hear of it in time. The Internet has changed all that, because it only takes one member of one of those sub-loops to post a sighting and instantly the entire birding world knows about it.

When I was chasing the Australian twitching record in 2002 I was constantly using the Net as a resource, particularly the website Birding-aus (*see* BIRDING-AUS). While it netted me (no pun intended) several ticks for my year list, it ultimately blew out my budget as I would drive miles out of my way to check into some outback motel just so I could plug my laptop into a phone line to check the Net. (And the lure of an actual bed figured somewhere in my decision, I am sure.)

It's not just twitchers who benefit. The Internet offers the opportunity for information to be shared and exchanged at hitherto unprecedented speed, which can help the cause of conservation. The mass slaughter of migrating birds by hunters in Malta, the threat of clearing a crucial habitat for the Mallee Emu-wren for a toxic waste dump in Victoria, the impact of long-line fishing on albatross in the Southern Ocean; they can all be instantly communicated to a worldwide audience who can then organise to take action. Trends in bird populations that otherwise would not emerge until years down the track can be flagged with a simple query about whether other people have noticed a decrease in cuckoo numbers this spring, or an increase in cockatoo sightings in the suburbs.

While the Internet is undoubtedly a brilliant tool for the birdwatcher, there are several downsides that I feel duty-bound to alert you to. This is not the usual advice to watch out for viruses and Trojans, or warnings about responding to ads that ask if you want a larger penis; I'm talking about pitfalls specific to birding.

1. Don't believe everything you read

In the pre-Internet past, dodgy sightings seemed to have been generally filtered out before they reached the broader public, saving the rest of us many a wild-goose chase. If someone made an extravagant claim, it would usually be queried somewhere along the line. Now, with a hasty click of the send button, any claim is out there in the public domain.

Of course, mistakes on the Net can also be corrected instantly (and it is remarkable how quickly the vultures of scepticism gather over the vulnerable fawn of an unusual sighting): misleading information can be rectified and notice given of when a rarity has buggered off, all in an instant, thereby saving a lot of grief for those who were contemplating going for it.

2. The masters of their domain

The maxim that 'Those who can, do and those who can't, teach' could be readily adapted to the Internet; those that can are out there doing it, those that can't are on the Net talking about it. You have to wonder sometimes when the prolific Net jockey finds the time to go outside and do some actual birdwatching. Once upon a time birders proved their bona fides by getting out into the field and finding birds; on the Net the chief criteria seem to be access to a high-speed modem and a preparedness to comment on any topic that arises.

3. Looking for Mr Goodbar-tailed Godwit

As in life, on the Net there are people who are considerate, eager to help and willing to share. Then there are those who are simply out for whatever they can get. Thus they will appear to be your best online mate when you have access to some information on a bird they want to see, but once they have milked you for everything they need from you about that godwit sighting, you will never hear from them again.

Conversely, if you are someone who relies on the online birding community for information on where to find birds, you will inevitably have to reciprocate somewhere along the line, and if you have any sort of conscience you will do so, no matter how trivial the request is. This means the Internet can be a huge time-waster. I find much of my day online is answering correspondence that in normal circumstances I would never be involved in. Poetic justice, I suppose – he who lives by the Sword-billed Hummingbird dies by the Sword-billed Hummingbird.

4. In a democracy, the vote of the duffer has the same value as that of the genius

Science is elitist. It privileges the opinions of those who have considered their views, researched and tested them and then presented them before their peers for verification. The Internet, by contrast, is democratic. Every idiot has a voice. And on the Net it can be extremely difficult to work out who are the idiots spouting superstition, flights of fancy and untested assumptions, and who is talking sense. The best advice I can give is do not automatically assume that because somebody sounds authoritative they are in any way an expert on that particular subject.

5. Being spoonfed can damage your mental capacity

This may be me showing my age, but when I started birding I learnt by reading books, talking with more experienced birders and actually getting out into the field to see birds, hoping to find a few good ones for myself.

The Internet is a great place to learn, but just as the spellchecker and auto-correct function diminish a person's ability to spell words for themselves, I have noticed birders on the Net sometimes expect to have everything laid out in full detail for them and get very shirty when it isn't.

A typical example might go something like this:

INITIAL POST BY BIGTWITCH, TUESDAY 1030:
G'day all. There was a Spoon-billed Sandpiper at Werribee today.

[Actually, a Spoon-billed Sandpiper would hardly be announced so casually, as it would not only be a first record for Australia but would be for the uber-twitchers the most sought-after first there ever could be, due to a combination of its global rarity and it being on a par with a baby panda in terms of cuteness. But let's just assume for demonstration purposes that the message read as above.]

Within a very short time, there will be a barrage of questions along the lines of:

SPANGLED DRONGO [Many birders like to use a bird name as an Internet handle], TUESDAY, 1035:
Spoon-billed Sandpiper is not in my Australian field guide. Maybe you mean Royal Spoonbill?

BIGTWITCH, TUESDAY, 1038:
No, it is a Spoon-billed Sandpiper, a first for Australia. That is why it is not in your field guide.

SPANGLED DRONGO, TUESDAY, 1039:
What does it look like?

BIGTWITCH, TUESDAY, 1045:
A Spoon-billed Sandpiper looks a bit like a Red-necked Stint, about the same size but with a spoon-shaped bill.

SPANGLED DRONGO, TUESDAY, 1046:
So it is a wader then?

BIGTWITCH, TUESDAY, 1055:
Yes, it is a sandpiper, therefore a wader. You can pick it out from the other waders at Werribee because it is the only one there in breeding plumage. It has a red neck and chest. None of the others do.

SPANGLED DRONGO, TUESDAY, 1056:
Where is Werribee? I live in Melbourne, is that anywhere near Werribee? I do wish you would be more specific.

BIGTWITCH, TUESDAY, 1108:

Werribee is in Victoria, not far from Melbourne. Dozens of birders post their sightings from Werribee on this site every month.

SPANGLED DRONGO, TUESDAY, 1109:

When you say Werribee, do you mean Werribee township, the Werribee River, or Werribee Sewage Farm?

BIGTWITCH, TUESDAY, 1120:

Werribee Sewage Farm. Where all the waders are.

SPANGLED DRONGO, TUESDAY, 1121:

Where are the waders at Werribee Sewage Farm?

SPANGLED DRONGO, TUESDAY, 1127:

Bigtwitch? Did you get my posting? Where are the waders at Werribee Sewage Farm?

BIGTWITCH, TUESDAY, 1138:

All right, Spangled Drongo, listen up. From Melbourne you get onto the West Gate Freeway, go over the bridge past Werribee township and take the Point Wilson turn-off. Turn left into Paradise Road (see attachment for a map). If you don't have a permit and key already, you will need one (details on how to get one attached). Drive along Paradise Road, through two gates which you will need to get out and open and then close after you have driven through them. When you come to a large, shallow water body on your left, you should notice a large feeding flock of birds in the water. These are mainly stints but the Spoon-billed will hopefully be amongst them, standing out because it is the only one with a spoon-shaped bill, the only one that has any red on it and the fact that it will most probably have the telescopes of a dozen twitchers trained on it. So if you want to see it, I suggest you get in your car and go. Is that enough info? Any more questions, Drongo?

SPANGLED DRONGO, TUESDAY, 1139:

Where did I park my car?

6. Too much information

Often if you put a simple request or observation on the Net, you are going to be bombarded with more information than you could ever possibly need or want. For instance you might have seen a Great Crested Grebe on your local reservoir for the first time ever and thought it might be of interest to others.

INITIAL POST:

Hi, everyone. Today I saw a Great Crested Grebe at Local Patch Lake in southern Tasmania, the first I have observed in eight years birding here.

[Simple, you would have thought. The record is out there. Any southern Tasmanian locals who want to see it now know about it, and even if you never submit it on an Atlas form or to a rarities committee, it is now in the public domain. But then comes the unexpected avalanche.]

RESPONSE 1:

I saw a Great Crested Grebe there in 1991.

[OK, fair enough. It may have had an overtone of one-upmanship, but it shows that these birds have turned up there before, which in a sense helps the veracity of your record. But it doesn't stop there.]

RESPONSE 2:

I once saw five Great Crested Grebes on Lake Wendouree. This was in July 1973.

[OK. Not only is Lake Wendouree in another state, the sighting was two decades earlier. Not really too relevant, you would have thought.]

But this is only the opening of the floodgates. You will now have sparked a Great Crested Grebe pissing contest, with each contributor trying to somehow outdo the previous posting. If it is a slow bird week, you will end up with long missives about watching Great Crested Grebes courtship rituals seen in the moonlight on a Slovakian marsh.

Then there will be a response debating the use of the term 'marsh' for what is clearly an open body of water which will lead to a debate on at what depth a water body is officially deemed a lake, which will eventually end up in a debate about the merits of wader banding. Every email thread about birding ends up in a debate about wader banding (*see* WADER BANDING).

Isabelline Wheatear / a smallish bird that usually breeds in Central Asia and winters in India and East Africa.

Until November 2002, the closest an Isabelline Wheatear had ever come to Australia was a single sighting in Burma in 1980. Then, miraculously, one was discovered in a desolate cow paddock/sports field in the north Queensland town of Mount Carbine.

As a birdwatching experience, it was rather unedifying. Here was a plain brown bird in a barren field littered with a mass of dried cowpats. At times it was difficult to distinguish the bird from the turds.

But of all the birds I have on my Australian list, this is one of the most remarkable, for several reasons: 1) it was thousands of kilometres out of its range; 2) the fact that anyone bothered scanning such an obviously crappy piece of habitat; 3) it is so extremely unlikely to appear in Australia ever again, making it one of the most prized ticks in my entire list. This bird was like having Jimi Hendrix turn up on your doorstep for a jam, or the government declaring that they won't bother taxing you this year, or Angelina Jolie ringing up and asking if she can come around for a sleepover. Well maybe not that unusually good, but I have to say that the 800-odd bucks I spent on the cross-country flight from Broome to Cairns was certainly worth every cent.

Jabiru / a large, striking black and white bird, found across the northern half of the country, the Jabiru is Australia's only stork.

There is also a stork in South America that goes by the name Jabiru. As it was described before the Australian bird, scientific protocol dictates that the South American species gets custody of the name. Hence the Australian bird is now officially known as Black-necked Stork, though this has got quite a number of birders' noccies in a twist (oops, I just breached my edict about using the word noccies – *see* BINOCULARS).

Calling it an Australian Jabiru won't work either, because it also occurs in India and South-East Asia and to claim it as our own would be a bit of flagrant cultural imperialism. And so whenever a birder calls the bird one name or another, there is a flood of passionate debate about what it should be called. Birders are like that – they can't see the wood ducks for the treecreepers. (Actually, there was a similar furore when it was suggested that in order to avoid confusion with the American Wood Duck, ours be called the Maned Goose. But that's another story …)

Meanwhile, unaware of the controversy, the stork in question continues to go about the business of living with a stately elegance.

Jammy Pete / the kind of charmed birder that never seems to dip out on a bird – ever.

Jammy Pete is often the last guy to see a rarity before it disappears for good. Another half an hour and he would have missed it. But he never does, somehow he just seems to connect miraculously with the target species every single time. It is not that Jammy Pete is a gun birder; just that the cards always seem to fall his way.

The jammiest Pete I have ever witnessed was out at Werribee Sewage Farm on a bitterly cold day, where Victoria's first Yellow Wagtail had been reported. Another twitcher and I had been trying to locate it but the wagtail was not co-operating. Eventually we found it sheltering from the wind in a small copse of scraggly trees. As we approached it took flight and landed on the nearby road, directly in front of Jammy Pete's car as he was driving in. We had been out in the wind for hours trying to track the thing down and this guy had ticked it off before he had even got out of his car.

The antithesis of Jammy Pete is the birding Jonah, the type of unhappy sod who seems to pack a heavy dose of bad luck every time he goes birding. One such Jonah, a Werribee regular, was out looking for the wagtail when the same thing happened to him, sort of. This guy would have logged hundreds of hours in the field at Werribee that year and had not had a sniff of the wagtail. Another group of twitchers managed to locate the wagtail and could see his car in the distance. They tried signalling, but by the time he drove over to them, the Yellow Wagtail again took flight onto the road. As with Jammy Pete, the bird landed in front of his car, but this bloke didn't see it and drove over it. Luckily the wagtail survived and after another couple of tortuous hours he did finally manage to get a look at it. By this time Jammy Pete was away in the pub celebrating yet another successful twitch.

Jizz / the indefinable quality of a particular species; the 'vibe' it gives off that aids in identification.

T. A. Coward, the first person to use the term in print, summed it up well in 1922 when he said it was about 'character, rather than characteristics'. Jizz is what the gun birder goes by in identifying a bird that they have seen out of the corner of their eye while driving along the highway at 110 kilometres an hour. Not surprisingly, jizz is often viewed with suspicion, being dismissed as a kind of birding alchemy, but it is amazing how often a good birder will correctly identify a bird on the basis of the hunch they have developed from a bird's jizz.

Jizz can be a more reliable method of identification than, for example, the patterning of the feathers. Feathers can vary between individual birds, and some may be missing or stained or damaged. Jizz is more directly affected by the way a bird is physically put together. For instance, a bird with longer wings will not need to flap them as quickly as a bird with shorter wings to maintain the same velocity. An eagle can be distinguished from a falcon because the falcon has narrow, streamlined wings, compared to the eagle's broad, thermal-catching wings. So by a technical reading, the two can be separated according to the shape and length of the respective wings; alternatively, using the concept of jizz, you would notice that the falcon flew fast and direct whereas the eagle circled on thermals in a much more lazy (or imperious) manner.

So jizz can be a useful tool for identifying birds. But be warned: because it invokes such imprecise terms as 'lazy' or 'imperious', jizz is incredibly subjective. A rare sighting would never be accepted purely on the basis of jizz alone, and to rely completely on jizz to identify a bird leaves you open to accusations of 'majizzmo' (*see* MAJIZZMO).

Julatten / a tiny village in far North Queensland; one of the sacred sites of Australian birding.

Julatten has a school, a couple of houses and that's about it. But it does have a caravan park, now rebranded as Kingfisher Park Birdwatchers Lodge. For more than four decades, this has been the place to go for many of the region's specialties such as Lesser Sooty Owl, Blue-faced Parrot-finch, and particularly Red-necked Crake. Until very recently, Julatten was the only generally known site for this elusive rainforest species. Since at least the 1960s, a birding rite of passage has been to set yourself up by the park's rainforest pool at dusk to wait for the normally terminally shy crakes to emerge from the gloom and put on their show.

Jumping the gun / blurting out what you think a bird may be based on your initial impressions, no matter how misguided they turn out to be.

Though it may seem like a bad thing, there is no shame in jumping the gun. At worst it can lead to a massive ribbing from your companions when you call a Peaceful Dove a Scarlet-chested Parrot, but it is far better to suffer momentary embarrassment than have the entire group miss out on a Scarlet-chested Parrot due to your reticence to call something.

Someone mindlessly blurting out the first bird name that pops into their head can, however, become bloody annoying, particularly if they make the same mistake repeatedly. And being caught in the crossfire of competing egos when two people are both jumping in to be the first to nail a correct ID and thereby prove their moral ascendancy can make you want to pull their binocular straps tight around their necks until their eyes bulge like a Marbled Frogmouth's. But what I find far more objectionable is the opposite end of the equation: the birder who acts like a Mississippi riverboat gambler, with cards held so tightly to the chest they will have to be pried from their clasping fingers before they can be buried. I have heard of boat trips (*see* PELAGIC) where, after several hours at sea, someone will call a bird such as Antarctic Prion only to be told, 'I've been seeing them all day.' This is incredibly frustrating if you are the one charged with logging the day's birds; catastrophic if you have forked out for the trip specifically to see an Antarctic Prion. Such behaviours can arise because the birder is so wrapped up in the birds they are seeing that it doesn't even occur to them to share them with their companions, or simply because they are a character who likes to have the last word on everything. They will wait until everybody else has laid their cards on the table to see whether they can trump them.

Such a strategy is high risk, because if the cards are held to the chest too long, the bird in question may have flown. This isn't a good look for the claimant, for if it occurs too often any future claims will be looked upon with suspicion. At times, I wonder whether the relevance deprivation syndrome is so strong in such personalities that they would even resort to stringing a sighting just to get one up on their rivals, a bit like a healthy kid faking an illness when they feel their siblings are getting too much attention from their parents (*see* STRINGER).

Kakadu / a huge national park in the Northern Territory.

So often a place that is touted as a bird lover's paradise falls far short of the mark for the hardened birder – a few ducks in a pond does not a paradise make. Kakadu National Park is one of the very few places that really does live up to the hype.

Much of the attraction of Kakadu is its immense size. Covering almost two million hectares, Kakadu is larger than 78 countries including Fiji, Lebanon and Singapore. Kakadu includes a vast array of habitats from mangroves, swamps and open floodplains to woodland, patches of monsoon rainforest and rocky escarpments. No wonder over 280 species of bird are regularly seen there, including Banded Fruit-Dove and White-throated Grasswren, both of which are found almost nowhere else on Earth.

But Kakadu is not indisputably *the* best birding site in the country. Being over 200 kilometres long and 100 kilometres wide, it is bound to have a large species tally. If you were to draw a radius of 100 kilometres around any major coastal city, you would probably end up with a species total on a par with, or even higher than, Kakadu's. More than 360 species have been observed in the Sydney region alone; Werribee Sewage Farm, which is 1/200 the size, boasts a list almost as long as Kakadu's.

Many a local council or conservation organisation is guilty of milking figures like this to give a distorted picture of the conservation value of their particular patch. So any time you read of some local wetland or region boasting that it has 'as many birds as Kakadu' you know what size grain of salt to take with the statement. They may be technically correct, that over the years the same number of species have been recorded, but it is a deadset certainty that the birds there are not going to be in the sheer profusion that is typical of Kakadu (and this time it is permissible to use the term 'dead cert' – *see* DEAD CERT).

Kalkadoon Grasswren / a small bird of the rocky, spinifex-clad slopes of western Queensland, until very recently thought to have been an isolated race of the Dusky Grasswren. Studies have revealed the Kalkadoon Grasswren to be a distinct species and all reports suggest it will be accorded such status when the new checklist comes out (*see* CHECKLIST, SPECIES, TAXONOMY).

Because grasswrens are so difficult to see, having made a habit of living in remote and inaccessible habitats, the 10-Grasswren Club is probably more exclusive than the 700 Club (*see* 700 CLUB). I can only claim to have seen eight, a fact that would have me mercilessly teased at the Twitchers Club Lounge, if such a thing existed.

Of course, merely being rare or of scientific interest doesn't assure a bird a place in this book – there always has to be some controversy, and with this little creature, it is the very name Kalkadoon. Some people disagree intensely with the name, claiming that a more appropriate name would be the Ballara Grasswren after the site where it was first discovered; the Selwyn Grasswren, after the Selwyn Range where the bulk of the population can be found; or Horton's Grasswren in honour of the discoverers of the bird.

Some argue that the Kalkadoon people after whom the bird is named may not have had any actual connection with the bird, and that their traditional territory didn't substantially overlap with the habitat of the grasswren. But this view may have initially arisen because the anthropologist who recorded the words for birds from the Kalkadoon language wouldn't have known to ask about the grasswren as he would never have seen it. And so the debate rages.

Meanwhile, the grasswrens themselves continue to hop about the boulder-strewn slopes, slipping out of view whenever a birder approaches.

Kookaburra / an iconic Australian species, the largest members of the kingfisher family.

There are actually four species of kookaburra, two of which are found in Australia, the others being confined to New Guinea. The Blue-winged Kookaburra has a pretty incredible sounding call, but it is the Laughing Kookaburra that is the famous one, being one of the best-recognised Aussies throughout the world. Yet, as a kid, I thought there must be kookaburras all over the world because they would turn up on all sorts of Hollywood soundtracks for movies set in all manner of exotic country, particularly the Tarzan movies and television series.

It was quite confusing really. There would be Tarzan, a white guy, supposedly in Africa, often hanging around with a little Latino kid who I swear was a pre-pubescent Cheech from Cheech and Chong. And they would run around a Hollywood back lot to the sound of Australian kookaburras and Indian peacocks with South American macaws fluttering about as they wrestled African Lions. Welcome to globalisation, son.

Leeton / a small irrigation town in the Riverina District of New South Wales; home to Australia's first birdwatching fair.

Punching well above its weight, little Leeton stole a march on many larger centres by developing the Australian Birdfair, a sort of caravan and camping show for bird-nerds. Inspired by the famous British birdwatching fair in Rutland that draws a crowd of near 20 000, the inaugural Leeton event in 2006 attracted closer to two hundred punters, perhaps due to the town's distance from the capital cities. But the tenacious committee have committed to persevere and with both Birds Australia and BOCA supporting the event, there is every chance that it could catch on, particularly as Leeton sits adjacent to Fivebough Wetlands, one of the most productive inland swamps for waterbirds in the country. If Rutland can be described as the Glastonbury of British birding, then Leeton may well become the Sunbury of Australia's birding scene, (hopefully without the nudity!).

Lifer / a new bird for a birder's life list; also known as a tick (*see* TICK).

It is said that former Australian cricketer Glenn McGrath could name the batsman and circumstance of every one of his test match dismissals. Similarly, a lifer is so significant to the twitcher that if you throw a random number their way they'll respond, 'Bird 625 – White-eared Monarch, Feb 13, 2002, Lacey's Creek near Brisbane'.

Upon seeing a lifer, the correct protocol is to turn to the person next to you (or to nobody in particular if you are birding alone) and describe a large tick with your arm as you declare in an exaggerated, drawn-out American accent, 'Lifer!'

The other alternative is, with a great flourish, to stick your two index fingers outward in the manner of an AFL goal umpire and emphatically pronounce the word 'Goal!' like a sports broadcaster.

There is no real reason behind this, and you will look like a total dropkick when you do, but hey, you've just seen a lifer, so what do you care what people think?

List / for some birders, probably just as important as the actual birds on the list; also *see* CHECKLIST.

One of the main criticisms of twitchers is that, for them, the majesty, beauty and wonder of a bird become meaningless, reduced to a mere tick on a list. Twitchers aren't alone in this regard. I have been on a boat where the seabird researcher on board, realising he was only a few birds short of banding his hundredth Wedge-tailed Shearwater for the day, busted his chops trying to net those last three or four more in as manic a fashion as a shopper at a Boxing Day sale rushing the whitegoods section (*see* BANDING).

There is only one thing that brings a twitcher greater joy than seeing a rare, endangered species for the first time, and that's writing its name down in his list. And I say 'he' deliberately, because it is interesting that most twitchers are men. Men love to make lists. Women love to make lists too, but they actually use them for practical purposes, like shopping lists, lists of chores, or lists of insensitive things that their partners have done that can be used in arguments weeks, months, even years later.

Lists are great for guys because it's a way of conquering something without any actual physical confrontation. You don't have to tackle anything to ground, shoot it with anything, or hurt it (or have it hurt you) but you have conquered it no less, because it is down on your list, and has been categorised by you. Sure, a cassowary may have the power to slice your bowels in two with one kick of its powerful claws, but you have discursive dominance over it because it is now down on your list.

One of the great attractions of lists is that they give you a sense of control in an otherwise chaotic and baffling universe. By making a list, you order the world, and more importantly, you can work out where you fit into it. It's much easier to work out who you are by working out what you're not. Think about it: whenever you've done something really bad, really shocking, haven't you justified it by comparing yourself to someone even worse? 'Well, sure I spent the rent money on grog, but at least I don't go round clubbing baby seals.' 'Yeah, I slept with your sister while you were in labour, but at least I'm not Demir Dokic.' No matter how disgusted with ourselves we get, there's always someone we can feel superior to.

 ACTION: If you haven't already tried it, start up a bird list. Any list. It could be a life list, or a year list, or a day list. It might be a state list or a local patch list, or even a list of target birds you would most like to see. You will find that by opening yourself up to the world of lists you exponentially expand the opportunities to spend time on birding, and you can watch your productivity and the quality of your relationships go downhill correspondingly.

Listeria / an all-consuming, pathological obsession with lists, where the list itself matters more than the actual birds.

A friend of mine was sitting on the porch of a birding lodge in the rainforests of Ecuador watching a myriad of hummingbirds come into the feeders when an American tour group rocked up. As the tour leader enthusiastically shouted out the names of all the species that he could identify, members of the (predominantly retirement-age) group dutifully ticked off those species in their checklists. Some of them never even looked up to see an actual hummingbird! It's the birdwatching equivalent of the tourist spending all their time at the Taj Mahal or the Louvre with their nose buried in the guidebook, rather than actually looking at the thing they have come to see. I know of one birding guide who once tried to show a visiting overseas birder a Fawn-breasted Bowerbird on Cape York. The bird flew off before the visitor could see it, whereupon his only question to the guide was, 'Did you see it well enough for me to tick it?'

Like its medical namesake, Listeria can be very hard to eradicate. Sufferers can find themselves making lists about every aspect of their lives, from the amount of times they have eaten chicken in the past month (and then comparing with previous months' chicken-eating figures) to the number of people they have slept with, leading to a tendency to shout out declarations like 'I love you, number 37!'

The author would just like to point out that the above quote is not from personal experience. If I was to shout out like that, the number would, of course, be far higher.

List of lists / something someone with Asbirders Syndrome is likely to make.

Here is a list of some of the more stupid lists I have heard that people have kept:

1. List of birds a birder has dipped on.
2. List of birds seen on television.
3. List of birding personalities seen.
4. List of birds seen copulating.
5. List of birds seen while copulating (the birder, not the birds).
6. List of birds seen copulating while the birder is copulating.
7. List of birds seen in dreams.
8. List of nuts eaten while birding. (The goal is to become a member of the Ten Nut Club.)
9. List of birds that a birder's can of beans has seen. (The can was lent out to other birders and ended up having a bigger list than its owner.)
10. List of lists made.

Literature / a form of writing involving the use of the imagination and a focus on the beauty of language and its emotional effect – clearly of no use to the birder, who would much prefer an Elegant Tern to an elegant turn of phrase.

There are, however, a number of books about birds and birdwatching that, while not being field guides, are nevertheless such cracking good reads that they may interest even the most severe Asbirder. I particularly enjoy fishing out old accounts of birders' rambles in the pre-Internet and mobile phone twitching era, but there are some truly great books written about birding in the contemporary era. Some of the best I have come across include:

Little Black Bird Book by Bill Oddie, the 1999 reprint of which was, paradoxically, white, is still by far the funniest book about birding culture I have read. Well worth a read, though if you could skip over the bits where I have stolen his jokes, it would be much appreciated.

Birders by Mark Cocker, while not possessing the same level of humour as Bill Oddie's book, is a brilliant insight into birding culture liberally sprinkled with some classic tales of some seriously nut-job British birders.

Kingbird Highway by Kenn Kaufman recalls his amazing journey on the road as a seventeen-year-old hitchhiker in the early 1970s trying to break the North American Big Year record. It is a good thing I only discovered this book in my mid-30s, as if I had read it as a teenager I would most probably have been out the door with my binoculars there and then.

The Big Year: A Tale of Man, Nature, and Fowl Obsession by Mark Obmascik uses the author's journalistic background to stylishly recount another American Big Year attempt. Taking a more objective view, he follows the travails of three mad-keen birders who inadvertently find themselves in competition with each other to break the record.

A Bird in the Bush: A Social History of Birdwatching by Stephen Moss is a beautifully written account of how birdwatching evolved into such a massive pastime in England. The passages on birders fighting in the trenches of World War One are some of the most moving evocations of the battlefield I have read

And, of course, it would be remiss of me not to mention *The Big Twitch*, written by some joker who reckons he saw 703 species in Australia in the one year (my publisher threatened to rock my roof every night unless I mentioned it).

Local patch / a likely looking area of bush or swamp within easy access of your home, where you can go birding on a regular basis so that you can monitor the changes in the local bird population over time.

One of the best things that you can do for yourself as a birdwatcher is to adopt a local patch – even if you already have many ticks on your list, there is always the chance that something new may turn up for your local list. And while you may never become the number-one authority in any other field, the chances are that if you start regularly birding your local patch you will soon become the resident expert by default. Choose a patch that is not too popular with other birders; if you adopt somewhere as popular as Werribee Sewage Farm, know that you will have to compete with a whole gaggle of serious birders for the exalted title of local expert.

There is another benefit of local-patch birding that has little to do with bolstering a birder's fragile ego. You can actually have an influence on conservation decisions. I began my birdwatching career at Seaford Swamp, so after twenty-plus years there was probably no one who knew the place more intimately. When Melbourne Water took over management of the swamp and was keen to improve the habitat values, I was consulted on the process and, as the area had been in drought for ten years, I was the only one who had been around long enough to point out where, in a wet year, the wetland areas would be, thereby saving them from being revegetated with inappropriate plantings that would have destroyed important wetland habitat. So as the wise old saying goes, every expert needs a local patch and every local patch needs an expert.

Lorikeets / a gregarious and noisy group of parrots with brush-tipped tongues adapted for feeding on nectar; six species of lorikeet are found in Australia.

The brightest and most gaudy of the lot is Rainbow Lorikeet. I have witnessed a British twitcher straight off the plane, tearing up with joy at seeing such glorious birds so easily, for the Rainbow is also the most conspicuous of the lorikeets and can be easily found in every state capital, making it one of our most well-known native birds.

In some ways lorikeets conform to the stereotypical Aussie character, particularly the young Aussies that you encounter anywhere around the globe where there is a train station and a backpackers bar. They are brash and aggressively sociable, and have a tendency to get on the grog. The phrase 'as pissed as a parrot' must surely come from lorikeets. Sometimes the nectar that they feed on actually ferments in the hot sun and you will find lorikeets staggering about below the food trees, with their wings around their mates singing the lyrics to Cold Chisel's 'Khe Sanh' or Hunters and Collectors' 'The Holy Grail'.

Magpie / one of the most easily identifiable birds, even to non-birdwatching Australians; an unpopular bird for reasons outlined below.

Continuing the trend of unimaginative names bestowed upon our native birds by English settlers ('robin' for a group of flycatchers unrelated to English robins; 'wrens' for a similarly different family of birds with only a vague resemblance to their British namesake), the Australian Magpie is really only very distantly related to the magpies of Europe. What it does share with its European counterpart is the ability to thrive in the conditions created by urban and agricultural development. The Australian Magpie is one of a small group of avian winners in this country.

If you asked an Australian to name ten birds that they could identify, the magpie would be right up there with the emu, eagle and kookaburra. But this doesn't make it Australia's most popular bird. Many know it because every spring, certain members of the species (but not all) become extremely aggressive, swooping all that come anywhere near their nesting territory. While no fatalities have been recorded, magpies have managed to draw blood on many an occasion. The best solution is not to enter their territory, but if that is unavoidable, wearing a helmet or hat with eyes drawn on the top is a good deterrent, as the magpie won't swoop if it thinks you are looking at it. This makes for safer passage and gives everyone else a laugh as you walk down the street wearing an ice-cream container with giant eyes staring up at the sky.

Another reason for the magpie's low reputation among the general public is that it is the mascot for the Collingwood Football Club, the side that the rest of the country loves to hate. They are actually the team I support, so for me the magpie is not a danger to the head, it is a danger to the heart – being the team that has lost more Grand Finals than any other in any national sport, the Magpie supporter's heart is regularly torn asunder.

Birds don't feature all that prominently in Australian sporting circles. I guess they just don't represent the same sort of aggression as Lions and Tigers and Bulldogs. Interestingly in a game that is far more aerially based, there are five bird teams in the AFL but only two in the NRL, a sport where the ball is conveyed across the field far more often at ground level, tucked under the arm of a Bronco, Shark or Dragon. When the national netball competition set up a few years ago, the teams were all named after birds. All very well, but I wonder whether Newcastle and Canberra supporters have any idea of what a Jaeger or a Darter is. And supporters of the Perth Orioles must be scratching their heads, as the closest oriole to Perth is more than 2000 kilometres away in Broome!

But I think this is an encouraging trend that will help get the bird message out into the public's consciousness. So, running with the Netball Association's lead, I have put some thought into a few new names that perhaps our football, basketball, cricket and other sporting teams might like to adopt in order to give some of our lesser-known or endangered birds a run . . .

The Perth Princess Parrots
The Brisbane Black-breasted Button-quails
The Murwillumbah Marbled Frogmouths
The Fremantle Freckled Ducks
The Cairns Cassowaries
The Northern Territory Night Parrots
The Hobart Hooded Plovers
The Orange Orange-bellied Parrots

And there is always politics. In the US the Democrats have a donkey as their mascot, the Republican Party an elephant. Perhaps our main parties here could adopt bird emblems, though how to work out which gets the galah and which gets the drongo could take some doing. Not to mention the coots, turkeys and geese.

Majizzmo / an affliction whereby a belief in their own ability to identify a bird solely on its jizz leads birders to cock up in a major fashion.

With experience, most birds can be identified from the most fleeting of glimpses (*see* JIZZ). But the problem with jizz is that it is far less immutable an identification tool than other aspects of a bird such as structure, plumage or even call, because at times birds don't look how you expect them to.

I have witnessed even the best birders caught out by their own majizzmo. One time at sea, a very good birder and I were discussing how a heavily hooded Hutton's Shearwater that we were both getting great views of could easily be mistaken for a much rarer Tahiti Petrel, a bird we had been lucky to see earlier in the day. A minute later, from another part of the boat, came a call of 'Tahiti Petrel!' The bird that we had been looking at was now rapidly disappearing over the horizon exactly where the gun birder was pointing. We yelled back, 'We've got a Hutton's out that way', and he replied scornfully, 'This bird has the jizz of a Tahiti Petrel'.

By the time he had seen the bird in question, it was several hundred metres away. I had previously marvelled at this ace's ability to correctly call a speck on the horizon a particular species and for it to be that species every single time. This guy knew seabirds better than any of us, but that knowledge led to a serious case of majizzmo that day and two Tahiti Petrels went onto the list when clearly there had only been one.

Unless of course, as he invoked, it was a case of the two-bird theory (*see* TWO-BIRD THEORY).

Mallee Emu-wren / one of our smallest birds, weighing in at only six grams. It would take four of these birds to equal the weight of the fat content of a single Big Mac.

These little critters are in serious trouble, due to the inability of their tiny wings to take them out of harm's way. Successive wildfires have all but wiped out this species in its former stronghold in South Australia; even birds that survive the flames are unable to reach distant pockets of remaining habitat. It now only occurs in any numbers in a few isolated patches of habitat in Victoria. But when the Victorian State Government was planning to build a toxic dump on the site of one of these colonies, the data that was being used to ascertain the conservation status of the species was out of date, not having taken into account the recent losses in South Australia. Luckily, the site was saved for other (primarily economic) reasons and the Emu-wren maintained its precarious toe-hold on the planet.

Migration / where birds move from one area to another (such as from their summer breeding areas to their wintering grounds), as opposed to sedentary birds (species that don't move far from their core range) or nomads (those that move about from place to place but with no regular, discernable pattern).

Australia has far fewer migratory birds than does the Northern Hemisphere. Many are as likely to be nomadic as they are migratory, a response to the harsh conditions of the Australian environment where unreliable rainfall means that, for much of the year, or even for years on end, a habitat is unsuitable for many species because of a lack of water.

The few migratory species we do have fall into four broad categories.

First, there are the Northern Hemisphere birds, such as the waders, that arrive here from their breeding grounds, in many cases from north of the Arctic Circle. Variants on this theme are some seabirds such as the Short-tailed and Sooty Shearwaters which breed here and then migrate to the North Pacific during our winter; a round trip of up to 20 000 kilometres.

Second, there is a further north–south migration of species that breed in Australia but tend to winter further north, particularly in New Guinea. Some of these species are partial migrants, in that only part of the population leaves our shores while the rest winter in north Queensland.

Third, some species are altitudinal migrants, breeding in the high country over summer and moving down to the lower hills and plains when it starts to get cold. Pied Currawongs and Flame Robins are two of the best-known examples. Some Tasmanian birds such as the Swift Parrot and the Yellow-tipped form of Striated Pardalote avoid the cold Tassie winter by heading over to the relative warmth of the mainland. Similarly, those of New Zealand's Double-banded Plovers that breed in the mountainous areas of the South Island tend to head over to Australia, while the rest of the population usually moves only as far as New Zealand's North Island.

Fourth, some species of Southern Ocean seabirds tend to visit our waters in the colder months. Though not traditionally regarded as migratory, as movement happens to some degree each winter when Antarctic seas freeze over, I would regard this as a form of migration.

An appreciation of bird migration fosters a greater appreciation of the rhythms of the land. Though it hardly equates to the thrill of the first spring cuckoo in Europe, I still get a kick out of seeing my first Flame Robin in winter, but maybe I'm just easily impressed.

Mother / the female parent; the one that traditionally takes on the bulk of the parenting, with the exception of emus, Button-quails and Britney Spears.

Generally mothers don't mind so much if their kids get into birdwatching. It gets the kids outside into the fresh air (if fetid swamps and sewage farms can be considered 'fresh air') and keeps them away from more dangerous pursuits like drugs and vandalism and merchant banking. All the same, my mum always had trouble coming to terms with my tendency to disappear for hours at a time when I took up birdwatching. I guess it can be a worrying enough habit in an adult, but not having a twelve-year-old turn up at dinner time when the last thing he said to you was that he was going down to a swamp . . . I see now that it might put a few grey hairs on a mother.

I doubt that she was any more comforted when I went birding with others, for here was her child heading off into God-knows-where with grown men who spent an awful lot of time hanging around swamps with binoculars around their necks, and who always seemed to be talking excitedly about boobies and tits and shags. God knows what she made of the phrase, 'We had a Fairy Tern down at the Mud Islands!' Even though it was a more trusting age than the hysterical nanny state we live in now, I am surprised I was allowed to get out with these guys as often as I did.

My mum was quite a talented artist and the payoff for her was that she had a ready-made companion and defender to watch over her on her landscape painting trips. She would set up her easel safe in the knowledge that I was in the vicinity birding. I don't know what she thought I would do if she were attacked – use my powers of honeyeater identification to stop the scoundrels? – but it gave her peace of mind.

In 1991 we took a road trip together, driving from Melbourne to Townsville to visit a close relative who was dying of cancer. I did most of the driving and would call out each new bird I saw, which she would duly note down in my trip list book. Mum contracted a fatal cancer herself not long after that, so we never got to make more such trips. I still value those names she wrote down in my book, not just because they are a connection to her, but also because they are about the only legible words ever written in any of my notebooks (*see* NOTEBOOK).

I don't visit my parents' grave as often as I would like, but when I do I make a note of the birds I see there. There have been some nice ones, like Eastern Rosella and Musk Lorikeet. I like to think they would enjoy having them there.

Moult / a process that all birds undergo at least once a year, replacing old and damaged feathers with new ones.

Sometimes birds, such as the Splendid Fairy-wren will moult into bright breeding plumage at the beginning of the nesting season. The differences between their breeding and non-breeding plumages can be as dramatic as those of Pamela Anderson with and without her make-up on.

Penguins have to come up out of the sea to moult, usually on their breeding islands. Nearly all of Australia's live vagrant penguin records are of young, inexperienced birds caught short away from their home island and having to haul themselves up onto the nearest beach. When it is a remote one and they are undisturbed they can happily sit there for the couple of weeks that moulting takes, living off accumulated body fats. Unfortunately, people who discover them mistake the bird's dishevelled state for illness and get the local wildlife authorities to take them into care, the stress of which is just as dangerous as anything that could be dished up on the beach. Usually the bird gets taken off to a zoo or wildlife shelter minutes before the first carload of twitchers arrives from Brisbane hoping to tick it off.

 ACTION: If you find a moulting penguin on a beach, leave it alone unless it is clearly unwell, or being harassed or holding up a sign saying 'Taronga Zoo or bust'; it is perfectly happy where it is. Try not to hang around it too long, not because you'll disturb it so much (after all, to a penguin we are taller, funny-looking penguins) but because you will be drawing its presence to the attention of unwanted human and dog-like predators.

New South Wales / the second smallest mainland state and site of Australia's first white settlement where a bunch of criminals were sent from England to guard some prisoners in 1788. Within a few years of colonisation, a property boom had occurred in New South Wales and rum had become the main currency. Not much has changed since, though rum is no longer the drug of choice.

With habitats ranging from deserts to rainforest and everything in between, and an impressive bird list of around 590, New South Wales rather surprisingly only has one endemic species, the Rock Warbler, which can be found in sandstone country on the outskirts of Sydney. New South Wales does have the biggest numbers of some very special birds such as Plains-Wanderer, Regent Honeyeater, Superb Parrot and Eastern Bristlebird.

There are some great birding areas along the coastline, such as Yamba and Dorrigo in the north, the Hunter Valley and Illawarra areas in the middle, and the Eden area in the south. There is some excellent inland birding to be had at places like the Capertee Valley, Deniliquin, Leeton and Sturt National Park. With the continental shelf coming so close to the coast, cities like Sydney, Newcastle and particularly Wollongong provide some of the best and most convenient pelagic birding in the world (*see* PELAGIC).

The birding organisations of New South Wales run their own race very well, and tend not to focus as much on the rest of the country. There are birding groups that have been operating quite happily for decades and nobody outside the state has ever heard of them. This is not so much because they are humble; it's more that (like most Sydneysiders) they know they are the centre of the universe so they don't need to worry about proving it to anyone. New South Wales has its own atlas scheme operating independently of the national one. Contrast this with the other state organisations, such as those in Victoria, which always seem to be competing to get Sydney's attention to prove that they are equals.

Birds Australia has a Sydney office and some regional branches, and BOCA has several affiliates throughout New South Wales, and then there are a host of other quasi-independent groups. The largest is Birding NSW, which has branches in Sydney and on the Central Coast.

 ACTION: Birding NSW can be contacted at www.birdingnsw.org.au/

Night Parrot / the grail bird of Australian bird-watching, the one bird that almost all twitchers most dearly want on their list; also the Australian bird around which the most myths and rumours abound.

For years, many people suspected that the Night Parrot might have been extinct, but unlike the Paradise Parrot – the only other mainland species believed to have become extinct since European settlement – relatively fresh specimens of dead Night Parrots have turned up, one in 1990, the other in 2006, both in south-west Queensland.

While travelling in south-west Queensland I heard more than one story of farmers who claimed to have Night Parrots on their property, but were refusing to tell the authorities because they feared their land would be compulsorily acquired for a national park. And apparently a couple of locals found a dead Night Parrot but wouldn't give it over to authorities because they wanted to mount it in the pub as a tourist attraction. Another rumour doing the rounds is that a state museum has a Night Parrot team on red alert and as soon as there is a definite sighting they will swing into action to collect specimens. A variation on this says that they also have a specially designed aviary waiting to start a captive breeding program. Yet another legend has it that the government (Queensland or Commonwealth, depending on which version) has purchased a property in western Queensland where Night Parrots have been sighted, and they have set up a high-security fence around it to keep intruders out. I imagine that the Night Parrots there share their habitat with Paradise Parrots, Tasmanian Tigers and Bunyips, all tended lovingly by their keepers Harold Holt and Azaria Chamberlain.

Unfortunately it is hard to distinguish fact from fiction, for like the Tasmanian Tiger or Bigfoot or the Loch Ness Monster, once people are told something is out there, some inevitably start to see it. I have no doubt that there are many claims of Night Parrot which are in fact genuine birds, but there are a number of species that could be mistaken for a Night Parrot, particularly as most views are brief and in the dark. To the untrained eye, birds such as Owlet and Spotted Nightjar could be confused with a parrot, as these night birds are smaller than most non-birders realise.

Because of the name, people could quite easily assume that any parrot they see in the desert at night is a Night Parrot. It is not even 100 per cent certain whether Night Parrots actually do feed at night. Some of the after-dark records may have been of birds moving in to a water source to drink, which is a trait of a number of desert parrot species, in particular the Bourke's Parrot (also rare), and even the common Budgerigar.

So what should you do if you think you have seen a Night Parrot? Freak out is the first thing that comes to mind. Not merely because the sighting is a Night Parrot, but because it would set off a whole chain of highly-charged events. First, you would have to prove that the bird was genuine, a very difficult proposition if a photo is not obtained. Even just to report a Night Parrot sighting raises all sorts of ethical issues. If the location is publicised, then organised, thorough searches can be made; others will get the opportunity to share the magic and learn more about the bird and its habitat requirements. (And if the guys from the outback pub have it right, it would be a great boon to the local economy of the nearest towns.) On the contra side, you'd have to be worried about an army of twitchers descending on such a rare bird in a potentially fragile habitat. Not to mention boffins and museum collectors, as well as those seeking to take advantage of the huge price that would be offered for a specimen or eggs on the black market (*see* EGG COLLECTING).

Truthfully, I am not sure what I'd do if I saw one, but I think that ultimately somebody should be notified, be it the relevant wildlife agency, government department or Birds Australia who have put some resources in the past into the Night Parrot, and currently through their Threatened Species Network.

 ACTION: If you do see a Night Parrot, let me know about it. As soon as humanly possible.

Northern Territory / Australia's most sparsely populated region renowned for harbouring incredible wildlife and, if you believe movies like *Wolf Creek*, the bodies of hundreds of missing backpackers.

The Northern Territory has a wealth of birdlife, including four endemics and another six species that it shares only with the nearby Kimberley region in Western Australia. Essentially the Territory divides into two regions, the wetter, monsoonal Top End in the north and the arid zone further south. Both regions have birds that are really hard to get onto elsewhere in the country.

The area around Darwin provides superb birding with places like Holmes Jungle Swamp, Buffalo Creek and Sanderson's Sewage Ponds, one of the most outstanding in the country. (Where, as you are checking out the waterbirds and Asian vagrants, you will be sharing the view with the plant's very own resident crocodiles.) Further out in the Top End, Fogg Dam and the legendary Kakadu are very rewarding, but so are lesser-known areas around Katherine and Timber Creek. Down south the entire MacDonnell Ranges provide superb birding amongst even more superlative scenery, while it is amazing what turns up at the Alice Springs Sewage Ponds.

Because of its small population base, laced no doubt with a dash of that independent, pioneering spirit that Territorians still pride themselves on, there is no actual birding association per se in the Northern Territory. Birding in the territory is still primarily a case of various individuals heading out on their own. There are two field naturalists clubs in operation in the Territory, both of which have a strong birding component.

ACTION: The field naturalist clubs can be contacted at:
Northern Territory Field Naturalists' Club
P.O. Box 39565 ,
Winnellie, NT 0821
www.geocities.com/ntfieldnaturalists/

Alice Springs Field Naturalists
PO Box 8663
Alice Springs, NT 0871
www.geocities.com/alicenats

Notebook / some gear freaks get all fetishistic about what they write their bird notes in, but ultimately it doesn't matter what you use, as long as you get your sightings written down in something that you can refer to later.

A friend who was relatively new to birding obviously thought there was more to my choice of notebook than there really was, for one day he produced a $1.98 Spirax notebook and proudly waved it in the air, saying, 'See Dools; I've got the same notebook as you!' I didn't have the heart to tell him that I only arrived at that style by default. They are not waterproof, the spiral binding often comes loose at one end, jagging in your pocket, and come to think of it, they don't really fit into a typical size pocket and, as I refuse to wear my anorak unless it is bucketing down (*see* ANORAK), I have to jam the notebook into my inadequate jeans pocket, which creates the risk of ripping out a page or two. It is just that I have got used to them.

And I am happy to write my notes with a humble ballpoint pen. Some people have special pens; others prefer pencils. I find pencil tends to fade and I never remember to sharpen them. Some get around this by using retractable pencils, though I am put off by the story of one twitcher who, out in the bush, used this type of pencil to remove wax from his ears. The lead broke off and he had to go to hospital to have it surgically extracted. This didn't stop him from twitching, and after the operation he immediately checked himself out and went back out into the scrub to look for his target species (I think it was a Western Whipbird). Groggy from the anaesthetic and still unbalanced from having something bouncing around in his middle ear, he lurched from shrub to shrub, but still managed to see the whipbird.

The important thing is that you have a notebook and use it. Very few people have photographic memory, and even if they do, they are not going to be able to write down every detail hours or days after seeing something. Even if someone had a photographic memory, I would challenge their ability to transcribe accurately the intangible, such as jizz (*see* JIZZ), overall impressions, how the observer felt about what they were looking at, and so on. Writing observations down in a notebook is also a far more effective way of learning about birds than simply being told what you are looking at, either by another birder or a field guide.

And even more important is to get those notebooks transcribed or ordered in such a way that the information in them can later be shared with others. Even today, the bulk of birding knowledge in this country is stored not in journals or handbooks or field guides, but in the heads of the observers who get out there looking for birds. When such people die, a lifetime of information is lost. Having it jotted down in a notebook is a start to preserving all that collective knowledge, but if you are anything like me, it is totally illegible to anyone else and therefore ultimately of little value.

Actually, much of the material in my notebooks is also illegible to me. I decided to scan a particularly messy page from a notebook to see whether the computer could decipher it. All I could guess from the original was that it was a list of birds seen at Fivebough Swamp one morning in November 2006. Just before the hard drive self-destructed from confusion, it printed out the following . . .

FIRE DOUGH SWAP, MOVEBAMBI~//09@#--1045
Have a Sparrow 11
M.Bask 4#$
Red Wanker severed
Regurgitated Fly When
Swam Pea 2%
Bullion is Grate @!

And so it goes. I suspect that what the original actually did say was:

FIVEBOUGH SWAMP, NOVEMBER 24 0905- 1042
House Sparrow 11
M. Lark 4ad*
Reed Warbler – several
Variegated Fairy-wren
Swamphen 20
Baillon's Crake (H)*
* [Where 'ad' means 'adult' and (H) means 'heard only'.]

Actually, looking at it again, I think I did mean Fire dough Swap Move Bambi and the rest. It was a very hot day and I forgot to bring a hat.

 ACTION: Once you have come to the end of your notebooks, make sure you store them in a fire-and-flood proof container. One pioneer of the twitching scene lost all his notes in Cyclone Tracy, including details of many claimed firsts for Australia.

Nudity / not usually relevant to birdwatchers (there is nowhere to keep your notebook, for starters), but there have been birdwatching occasions when nudity raised its ugly head (so to speak).

In 1997, an Asian migrant, the Blue Rock Thrush, overshot its usual migration route by a couple of thousand kilometres and ended up on a rocky headland near the holiday resort town of Noosa in Queensland. People thought that the bird might have been disoriented or dislocated by the massive forest fires in its Indonesian wintering grounds. As it was a first for Australia, scores of twitchers naturally descended upon the headland. Most of them eventually ticked the bird off and went home happy.

Not so happy were the locals, as the headland the thrush temporarily called home was directly above Noosa's nudist beach. The sudden appearance of hordes of men armed with binoculars and telescopes was, as you could imagine, greeted with some alarm. Over the six weeks the bird was in residence, the police were called in regularly. The situation was not alleviated when one twitcher tried to explain his stalking presence away by saying he was only trying to get a better view of the thrush!

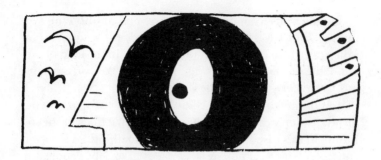

Observatories / establishments set up primarily for the study of birds in the wild.

Bird observatories have not flourished in Australia in the way they have in Britain. Birds Australia has made a stab at running observatories in the past but, disappointingly, over the past five years has closed two of them due to high running costs. The two that are left are both in Western Australia; one in Broome which, not coincidentally is right next door to Roebuck Bay, one of the key staging posts for tens of thousands of migrating shorebirds, and the other at the opposite end of the state at Eyre, on the edge of the Nullarbor Plain.

I believe Australia should set up bird observatories on places like Christmas Island, Ashmore Reef or in the Torres Strait. The Australian bird list would skyrocket as all that intense birding activity would undoubtedly yield a whole swag of new ticks for the Aussie list with birds that had overshot from Indonesia and New Guinea (*see* OVERSHOOTING).

One-eyed king / what you are when you are the only one who can answer: 'What bird is that?'

Whenever I was travelling with my dad and my uncle, they would ask me what bird it was they had just seen. As we were seeing the birds from our car, they were usually nothing too unusual and I was always able to answer the enquiries, to which my Uncle Pat would mutter the line, 'In the land of the blind, the one-eyed man is king.' (After Ron Barassi, Erasmus was Uncle Pat's favourite theologian.)

And though Uncle Pat could be an odd chap, becoming disproportionately excited whenever he saw a flock of sheep, I think in this case he was really onto something. As a birder you don't tend to get many advantages in society. People are more likely to make fun of you than look up to you. But they will inevitably come to you with a bird question. It would be a pity then, to let such moments slip away by mumbling. Seize the moment and be bold in your answer, regardless of whether you are 100 per cent sure or not. The chances are, you are going to be fairly close to the actual answer. The non-birder is not going to know the difference and probably won't retain what you say anyway, so where's the harm?

Of course it is foolhardy to attempt this when in any land other than that of the blind, for if you get the answer wrong you will end up looking quite the duffer. A friend of mine, a very good birder, was on a ferry trip across Port Phillip Bay with his family. On the way over he saw plenty of penguins in the water but the birder's father missed them. Coming back there seemed to be no penguins, until the very last minute when he saw a small black-and-white seabird, and loudly announced to all on the ferry that there was a penguin. At that precise moment the 'penguin' flew up from the water and out to sea, revealing itself to be a Fluttering Shearwater, rather more unusual in that area than a penguin, and the first that he had seen all day. Normally, his family would have no idea what a Fluttering Shearwater was and wouldn't have known or cared that he had got the ID wrong. But they all knew that a penguin cannot fly and so my friend's kingly status was shattered forever.

Orange-bellied Parrot / one of Australia's most endangered birds, the OBP (as it is known to birders) is a small, grass-green parrot with a habit of grabbing the headlines for all the wrong reasons.

In the mid-1990s when the Victorian State Government wanted to move Melbourne's major industrial chemical hub to one of the prime wintering sites of the OBP, the then Premier famously called it a 'trumped-up corella', implying it was little more than a pest species. (Corellas are a type of cockatoo that some Western District farmers are permitted to cull because of the damage they do to crops.)

Ten years later the federal environment minister vetoed a $220m wind-farm project, citing the protection of the OBP as his primary motivation. This would have been a wonderful outcome for the little parrot if they had ever occurred on the actual site. From a government that had previously allowed a wind farm to be constructed right next door to a site where the OBPs had actually been seen regularly, this was quite a turnaround in attitude.

The minister was roundly derided for using the parrots as a cloak for the real politics behind the decision, which had more to do with local horse-trading than conservation. Unfortunately, with a name straight out of a Monty Python sketch, the Orange-bellied Parrot became something of a laughing-stock, though the species did manage to last longer than the minister's career as he was demoted in the next cabinet reshuffle.

This would be about the only victory the OBP has had in the last 150 years. Never very common in the first place, its numbers crashed when much of its mainland saltmarsh habitat was cleared, to a point where now only around 140 birds survive in the wild. Only breeding in the remote south-west of Tasmania and migrating to the mainland for the winter, until recently the bulk of the population could be reliably found across three sites within a couple of hours' drive of Melbourne. For reasons unknown, the birds have largely abandoned these regular sites. Researchers know that roughly the same number of OBPs make it back to the breeding grounds but have no idea where around two-thirds of the population get to the rest of the time, and that is frustrating for both researcher and twitcher.

 ACTION: If you are really want to see an Orange-bellied Parrot in the wild and don't want to fork out for a helicopter ride (which is about the only method of getting to their breeding grounds) you can volunteer for the annual winter OBP counts. Covering all known sites OBPs have been recorded at, the survey teams also get into some areas that are normally off limits. But be warned, sightings are not guaranteed even on the official surveys. It took me seven surveys before I actually saw an OBP.

Ornithology / the scientific study of birds.

Scientists who get paid to study birds are called ornithologists. Almost everybody else interested in birds could be called amateur ornithologists, not that any birdwatcher would ever really call themselves such. Even the professionals tend to shy away from calling themselves ornithologists. All the ornithologists I've met are likely to claim they are scientists, researchers, or at a pinch, zoologists before the O word will pass their lips.

In fact, the only people that ever call me an ornithologist are the types of people that love to impress with their vast vocabulary. In calling you an ornithologist they are a) putting you down because it sounds a bit pompously daggy, and b) declaring to the world how clever they are by not only knowing such a big word but using it in what they think is the proper context. These are the type of people who call stamp collectors philatelists, actors thespians, and themselves onanists.

Outing / 1. an organised trip for birdwatchers. 2. a coming out of the closet for birdwatchers.

For far too many years I hid my shameful birding secret, but it meant that I was living a lie. It was only when I fully and publicly acknowledged who I was that I finally felt whole. The day I came out of the bird hide was the day I was truly free.

In this spirit I hereby unilaterally out some famous Australians whom I have it on good authority are closet birdwatchers. (Not that I have ever seen them out in the field or on any twitches. In fact, I doubt any of these people went to see the Grey-headed Lapwing (*see* GREY-HEADED LAPWING), unless they went incognito.) Well, after this list is published, they'll no longer need to go birding in false moustaches with their anorak hoods pulled down low!

I hereby out the following prominent Australians as closet birdwatchers . . .

Steve Abbott (the Sandman), comedian

John Doyle (Rampaging Roy Slaven), writer, comedian

Michael Veitch, actor, presenter

Max Walker, cricketer, author

Paul Sheehan, journalist, commentator (not the former cricketer and educator – oh bugger it, he's likely to be a birder too)

Paul Sheehan, cricketer, educator

Robyn Williams, science broadcaster, former extra on *The Goodies*, *Dr Who* and *Monty Python's Flying Circus* (not the American actor – oh bugger it, actually, no bugger the bugger it, that other Robin Williams probably is too, as are such international notables who have apparently confessed to being birdwatchers: Jim Jarmusch, Craig Newmark of Craigslist, Prince Charles, Princess Takamado of Japan, the Edge, Eric Clapton, Jarvis Cocker, Van Morrison, Jimmy Carter, Darryl Hannah and Damon Albarn)

Nicole Kidman, actress who just can't help going out with very short men.

Mel Gibson, actor, film-maker, amusing and witty drunk

Kylie Minogue, the singing budgie, or as she prefers to call herself, the singing *Melopsittacus undulatus*

Wolfmother, rock band, the members of which were conceived on the Led Zeppelin Down Under Tour of 1981

Skippy

Your favourite sports star

See, birdwatching really is cool. Everybody is doing it, so should you.

Overshooting / when a migratory bird, for whatever reason, keeps flying past its usual destination and ends up somewhere a long, long way further down the track, like Australia, for instance (*see* VAGRANT, REVERSE MIGRATION).

Not to be confused with when a bird such as Latham's Snipe or Freckled Duck is hunted almost to extinction.

Parabolic grot / one of the classic tales of Australian birdwatching but not a story for the faint-hearted, so look away now if you are squeamish or are reading this on board a boat.

Around 1982, a group of young birders was heading out to Wedge Light in the southern part of Port Phillip Bay to try and twitch Australia's first Cape Gannet, which had taken up residence there (*see* FIRSTS, FAST-TWITCH MUSCLES). The boat they had hitched a ride on was fairly small but very fast. One twitcher, a heavy smoker, sat on the bow choofing down one of his cancer sticks. Even for one so young the smoke was taking a toll on his lungs and he hoicked a particularly meaty oyster out to the side of the boat.

The spitball got caught in the boat's slipstream and, rather than heading out at right angles as intended, it traced a perfect parabolic arc around to the back of the boat, smack bang into the glasses of a young Scottish-born birdwatcher, who at first thought it was just a drop of sea spray. It wasn't until he turned around to the others that it became apparent he had been hit right between the eyes as the disgusting blob oozed down from his glasses.

The hilarity that ensued was not lessened in the slightest by his broad Scottish 'Oooh noo!' when he realised he had been hit, followed by the later claim that the grot was so disgusting, 'It tasted like sperm', with the *r* in sperm heavily rolled.

Whether or not this incident had a scarring effect on the individual concerned I can't say, but he had stopped birding within a couple of years of this. Suffice to say I am now very wary whenever anybody is on the bow above me when I am on a boat, particularly if they are looking a bit seedy. A parabolic grot is one thing, a parabolic chunder is another matter entirely (*see* SEASICKNESS).

Pelagic / 1. a type of seabird that feeds in pelagic waters (the open ocean). 2. an outing of usually demented birders on a boat out to the continental shelf and beyond to look for said pelagic species (*see* SEABIRDERS).

Pelagic outings can be an amazing wildlife experience, with majestic albatross and petrels, birds you hardly ever see from land, swarming around the boat. The flipside is that when the birds are off the boil, pelagics can be tedious in the extreme. I was on a pelagic off the north-west coast of Australia where we were out on the sea for five days. We saw some great birds including the little-known Matsudaira's and Swinhoe's Storm-Petrels, yet for hour upon hour we were lucky if we logged an individual of any species.

As a general proposition, I find pelagics uncomfortable and wet; and the threat of seasickness is a constant Banquo's ghost at the table of any enjoyment I might be having. Spending hours feeling queasy, bouncing around, getting covered in spray and watching other people throw up is not my idea of fun. Well, not since my Year 12 formal. Even though I've never actually vomited on a boat, I invest so much energy into worrying about whether I will be sick I can never relax enough to enjoy myself (*see* SEASICKNESS).

In the early days, if you wanted to go on a pelagic it was a case of approaching a fisherman in a coastal town and asking to hitch a ride out with him while he was on his daily run. Around the late 1970s birders got sick of missing out on good birds while the fisherman was hauling in his nets, and started to charter the boats themselves. Today there are regular pelagic trips in almost every state.

In these modern, litigious times, most commercial pelagics are run very professionally, as they need to be, for you are in one of the most alien environments for humans. As far as I'm aware there have been no major incidents or twitchers overboard on any Australian pelagics to date, but it must be remembered that the sea is utterly unpredictable and can throw anything at you at a moment's notice. I doubt the birders on a Japanese pelagic were quite expecting the military submarine that surfaced beneath their boat a few years back. Apparently all on board drowned. I don't know if this story is true, but it should be.

 ACTION: To find out more about when and where pelagic trips are being run, look up Tony Palliser's Pelagic Homepage: users.bigpond.net.au/palliser/pelagic/

Penguin / any of various flightless aquatic birds of the Southern Hemisphere, with webbed feet, and wings reduced to flippers; perceived to be lovable.

Eleven species of penguin have been recorded in Australia, though outside the sub-Antarctic Macquarie and Heard Islands, only one, the Little Penguin actually breeds here.

All the other species are vagrants, usually turning up dead as beach-washed specimens or when they get caught short of their home islands and have to haul themselves ashore to undergo moulting (*see* MOULT).

Penguins seem to be universally loved, and the penguin parade on Phillip Island is one of the country's biggest tourist attractions. The Little Penguin isn't all that uncommon around our southern shores, so there is little reason to visit the penguin parade, but whenever I have begrudgingly taken overseas or interstate visitors there I have been the one that they have had to drag away, as I get transfixed by their fascinating antics as they scamper up the beach to their burrows.

As I said, everyone loves a penguin, though the truth is that they are not nearly as lovable as is thought. As most penguin researchers will attest, they may look harmless, but you don't ever want to cross one. They are highly strung creatures, and will snap easily – a bit like birdwatchers themselves.

I bet you didn't know that about Little Penguins. They really are vicious. It wasn't a Chinese sub that took Harold Holt, it was Little Penguins. They were known as the Little Bastard Penguin until the Phillip Island Chamber of Commerce suggested a name that was more tourist-friendly.

Photography / something that non-birders assume that birdwatchers do when birding; nothing could be further from the truth.

Until recently I have never tried to photograph birds. There are two reasons for this. Firstly, photographing birds means that you have to stay with them, often for hours, lining them up for that perfect shot. Being that sedentary is not my idea of a good day's birding. The other reason is financial. In the days of shooting on film, bird photography was inordinately expensive. Not only did you need to buy a schmick camera with the best lenses available, but also the cost of film was prohibitive. For bird photographers, getting one top shot out of an entire roll of film was seen as a good day's shooting.

The digital camera has changed all that. Now with a decent memory card you can reel off hundreds of shots without a worry. A quick check of the screen on the back of the camera allows you to cull all the bad shots, and it costs you nothing in processing.

You don't even necessarily need a fancy camera any more. With digiscoping technology, where you essentially put the lens of the camera up to the lens of your telescope or even binoculars, you can get a reasonable close-up pic of a bird. There is all sorts of equipment available to make the process easier and give you more professional-looking shots, but for a record shot (a picture to show that you actually saw the bird) you don't need even these.

Even if you are a duffer with a digital camera, usually any shot can be blown up, or isolated, so as to be of value as a record shot. So ubiquitous are digital cameras now that a rarity report without an accompanying photo is almost looked upon suspiciously. A word of caution, though, with digital; because it is the computer deciding how to interpret the digital information it is being fed, it may make certain assumptions, particularly regarding shading. I have seen digital images of birds with areas of black that were not on the actual birds.

Some birders now spend so much time looking at birds through the viewfinder of their camera that they don't get a sense of what the bird was like in real life, in all its dimensions. They wait until they get home and look at birds on their computer screens before trying to identify them. Thus a bird that was clearly a Red-necked Stint when seen in the field, in natural light and among other birds for comparison, can become something 'unusual' when seen as a reinterpreted, pixelated image on a computer screen. In nearly all cases, if the bird didn't stand out as being different in the field, then it is not anything different, no matter what Mr Gates and friends' technology tries to tell you.

There are plenty of ways of upgrading or digitally altering images on a computer. This can be done for legitimate reasons: to crop or enlarge the image, to alter the shade or colour or grading to allow both clearer, more attractive images, and to be able to scrutinise particular features more clearly.

But with the technology comes the temptation to do a little extra fiddling. This can be done with innocent intentions, but once you start altering the truth (or the software's version of the truth) you are on a slippery slope that can easily drift into the area of fraud.

Alert to this possibility, international scientific bodies are now saying that they will not accept photographs alone as evidence of a species new to science. In Australia, just such a controversy is currently raging over claims of a new species of fig-parrot. The claimant has no other witnesses to back up his sightings but produced photographs of the alleged birds; these photos were instantly seized upon by the sceptics who have said they'd been digitally altered, changing a few of the facial features of a relatively common fig-parrot species, a claim backed up by an expert in the field of digital photography. It seems inconceivable that the claimant could have actually done such a thing, as he is a talented naturalist of great standing in many quarters, but with no other material or photographs as yet forthcoming, his claims are looking pretty shaky. One wag has suggested that, if it is a new species, it should be called the Photoshop Fig-Parrot.

But it is not just the birds that can be digitally altered. In other countries, rarities committees have knocked back claimed sightings of birds on the basis that, while they believed the bird itself was genuine, they didn't accept that the photo was taken at the location claimed. With digital technology it is now possible to take a photograph of a Bald Eagle, transpose it onto a scene with the Sydney Harbour Bridge in the background and claim it as a first for Australia.

Pishing / the art of expelling air, literally making a 'psh' sound in order to attract certain species of bird.

A variant of pishing is to purse the lips and suck air in, making a kissing noise, or to kiss the back of your hand or two fingers pressed to your mouth. All of these noises are alleged to imitate the agitation or distress call that some small birds make. Pishing can be surprisingly effective in bringing birds in close to the pisher as they investigate or come to the aid of what they think is a distressed bird. It is particularly effective in attracting thornbills, scrubwrens and some honeyeaters. It is not so effective in attracting a human partner, as there is no way you can pish and maintain any semblance of dignity at the same time. The first time I pished in front of my then girlfriend was on a beach holiday, where in the dune scrub I told her I could attract the Varied Triller that I thought was hiding just out of sight. The triller came in immediately. My girlfriend was suitably impressed, then politely but firmly requested that I never pish in her presence again. I haven't and we are married now, so let that be a lesson to all.

Plastic bag / something that is handy to have a couple of on hand whenever you are birding, particularly while driving or doing beach walks where you are more likely to come across dead birds.

Undoubtedly plastic bags are environmentally damaging, in both their production and the toll they take on wildlife once they are discarded. And popping a grungy seabird carcass into a plastic bag may get you looks of utter incomprehension from your non-birdwatching companions, but collecting dead specimens can be important in many ways.

For a start, you may need the corpse for later identification. There are a remarkable number of first records for Australia that have turned up dead, particularly after a severe storm or cyclone, and without the specimen (or at the very least several good photographs), these records would remain unconfirmed. Second, a well-preserved, undamaged specimen may be of interest to your state or local museum – it certainly saves them going out and killing a specimen of their own.

It is technically illegal for an unlicensed member of the public to possess wildlife, even when dead (or even a single feather), but if you are genuinely collecting a dead bird you have found to send on to a museum, you shouldn't be in any trouble. Usually. I know of one birder who shared a house with a pretty wild bunch. One morning the drug squad raided the property and although any narcotics had been successfully flushed away, they took a more than passing interest in what they uncovered in the freezer. With a fine at the time of up to $10 000 for every native bird kept without a permit, alive or dead, this twitcher was, for a while, staring down a fine of over $200 000 or years of jail time.

I can just imagine the twitcher's first day in jail. His cellmate, covered in tatts, barely pausing from his latest bout of self-mutilation, introduces himself as 'Bruiser', mass murderer, and asks Bird Boy what he is in for. 'Illegal possession of an Audubon's Shearwater'. Bird Boy may as well carve 'Bruiser's Bitch' on his forehead there and then.

Plastics / a rather dismissive name given to birds that have done nothing wrong except be introduced by unthinking or misguided humans into a land that they had not evolved in – that is, introduced, exotic species.

Plastics are so reviled because they can upset the ecological balance, and without the presence of natural predators that have evolved alongside them, their numbers can skyrocket.

In the past, many birders refused even to record them on their lists, a piece of birding snobbery or avian apartheid that made their historical spread and impact somewhat clouded. My view is that, once established, plastics should be counted on birders' lists as they have become, for better or worse, part of the biomass of an environment. And though they undoubtedly do cause damage and ideally should be removed, I find it hard to blame them. Some of them are particularly interesting species in their own right and ironically, some of the introduced birds such as Tree Sparrow and Skylark, are faring far better than in their land of origin, where changes to farming practices are causing their populations to crash. It is possible that one day the populations of such species will be replenished with stock from Australia.

Seeking out plastics for your list does, I admit, not quite have the same frisson as ticking off a native species, though it does take the avid twitcher to some interesting places: Rottnest Island for Common Pheasant and Peafowl, Norfolk Island for California Quail, King Island for all three, plus Common Turkey.

What constitutes a 'genuine' plastic is often a matter of contention. For a plastic to be accepted on the Australian list, it must have established a free-flying wild population for more than ten years. But often these criteria are hard to determine. For instance, I have seen Chukar Partridges on Flinders Island and Helmeted Guinea Fowl at Wyndham in Western Australia, both in the bush and seemingly running free. I guess I will have to wait and see whether anybody sees them ten years after my initial sightings before I can safely add them to my list. If it happens, it will be one of the more joyless ticks I have had, almost defeating the purpose of listing. Almost.

Playback / to many, an absolute birding no-no, akin to chopping down a rainforest tree with a sleeping panda cub in it, so that it falls into a river and crushes a dolphin that is swimming by.

While recordings of bird calls can be used to learn a bird's song, they can also be played back to attract birds, particularly male birds defending their territory through song. When they hear what they think is another male on their patch of turf, they are in like a shot to defend their honour – the avian equivalent of, 'What are you looking at, dickhead?'

While I normally don't like to side with the fun-stoppers, in this case I think the anti-playback brigade do have a point. In certain places in Africa and North America it is suspected that overuse of playback at specific sites has caused the rare owls that were constantly being called in to abandon their territories. The theory is that the birds were continually distracted by having to investigate the calls of phantom rivals and it took time away from their core owlish business of finding food for themselves and their families, so they eventually moved on to somewhere a little more peaceful.

With the scarcity of birders in this country, it is highly unlikely that the same situation is likely to occur very often, though authorities have banned playback at Two Peoples Bay Nature Reserve in Western Australia for fear that it will detrimentally affect the endangered Noisy Scrub-bird population. The key problem with playback is not so much that it disturbs the birds, but more the frequency with which it disturbs them. If a thousand birdwatchers a year wanted to see Noisy Scrub-birds and they all used tapes to attract them in, then (as this was until recently the only place to see these birds) it would mean an awful lot of distraction for the scrub-birds at Two Peoples Bay. Whereas if a thousand birders a year wanted to use playback to see a bird such as Barking Owl, the impact on individual birds would be much reduced, as there are scores of known sites for this bird around the country where birders can try to see them and, theoretically, any individual owls would not be repeatedly disturbed.

But birders, being as much creatures of habit as the object of their obsession, will often only try the same traditional sites when looking for a particular species. In Victoria the Barking Owl is a rare bird, though there is one pair near Chiltern that the general birding community have known about for many years, and it is these poor birds that are most often subjected to playback. But, as the birds are still there (and have successfully raised young) after more than 20 years, it would suggest that the level of intrusion is not so out of control as to cause them to abandon the site.

Who knows – seeing off those unseen interlopers may give the male Barking Owl a sense of bravado that makes him even more attractive to the lady owls.

Ultimately, I think that in every case where a birder is about to use a tape to attract a bird in, they should stop and ask themselves whether the benefit of seeing the bird is worth the disruption. In all honesty, usually it won't be, but I readily confess that I have used tapes in the past and probably will in the future. At times it has been as part of a survey to establish whether a species is present at a particular site. I can justify the intrusion by arguing that it is for scientific and conservation purposes, but there have been times where I have used playback purely so I, or the birders I was with, could get a view of the bird. I don't think us birders should beat ourselves up too much about occasionally disturbing birds in our quest to see them. There are so many other more serious threats to our birds and the occasional indulgent act on the birdwatcher's part is usually going to cause very little harm.

 ACTION: Calling birds in with the use of playback when they are breeding is even more disruptive, as there is the potential that a bird may abandon the nest, or predators may take the eggs or young while the adult bird is off investigating your taped calls. For most diurnal (daylight) birds the worst period is early spring, and for nocturnal birds such as owls, particularly in southern Australia, the critical period is in winter from late June through to August, so try to avoid using playback during these times.

Quail / one of the hardest group of birds to identify because they are usually only seen for an instant as they fly away from you.

We have three species of true quail in Australia: an introduced American quail, seven button-quails and the Plains-wanderer. Each group is not actually closely related to the others but when any one of them flushes from beneath your feet in an explosive whirr of wings, you tend to call 'Quail!'

I haven't seen the Buff-breasted Button-quail at all, and have only once had positively tickable views of King Quail, Plains-wanderer and Red-chested and Red-backed Button-quails.

A tip on how to get better views of quails is a little counter-intuitive. Once you have flushed a quail, watch where it lands (it will usually be a couple of hundred metres away) and then bolt straight for that spot. When a quail lands it usually then immediately runs through the grass into deeper cover. If you try and creep up on it, it will be long gone. By running directly to the spot, you may flush it again, but at least you'll be ready for it and there is a chance, if you slow up before getting to the exact spot, you might have a view of it frozen on the ground, trying to use its cryptic plumage to blend into its surrounds (so make sure you don't accidentally step on it).

Queensland / Australia's second largest and most northerly state, populated by Queenslanders who like to think of themselves as being different from other Australians, which is kind of ironic seeing that every second local you meet in Queensland originally comes from Melbourne or Sydney.

Queensland is the bee-eater's knees when it comes to Australia's birds. The state's bird list has passed the 630 mark, a far higher total than for any other state, but also substantially higher than any European nation (the UK has the largest list, with a little over 560). The Sunshine State has by far the most endemic species of any Australian state, with around 20 found nowhere else in the world and another 30-odd found nowhere else in Australia. So why the hell aren't we all up there birding right now?

Pull up anywhere on the Queensland coast that hasn't been developed to within an inch of its life and you will inevitably be in a great area for birds. Some of the really superb birding locations include Weipa, Bamaga and Iron Range on Cape York Peninsula, Julatten, Cairns, the Atherton Tableland, Townsville and Eungella in the north, the Conondale Ranges, Fraser Island, Lamington National Park and the area around Cunnamulla in the southern half of the state, to name but a few of the many contenders for the title of Australia's top Birding Paradise. From genuine 'beyond the black stump' desert to tropical rainforests, vast savannah woodlands and, of course, the islands and cays of the Great Barrier Reef, Queensland really does have it all in terms of habitat. And though we have done our best in recent decades to bugger it all up by clearing as much of it as possible, Queensland is still one of the greatest birding experiences in the world.

The main birding organisation is Birds Queensland (formerly the Queensland Ornithological Society) which is based in Brisbane. But Queenslanders being the sort of individualistic, non-conformist nutters that they are, have set up some very strong regional groups. And then there are the extreme individualists who operate outside any kind of group structure. Tucked away in their rainforest and desert lairs are the sort of renegade bushman-birders who make the Crocodile Hunter look like a Paddington Dandy. Such characters (and they are inevitably referred to as 'characters') have supernatural bushcraft skills, wear shorts so tight they would make an AFL footballer wince and seem to be able to survive on nothing but the undigested fruit they find in cassowary pooh.

 ACTION: Here are the contact details for many of Queensland's birding organisations:

Birds Queensland
    The Secretary, Birds Queensland
    PO Box 2273
    Milton, QLD, 4064
    birdsqueensland.org.au/

For the various BOCA branches around the state:
    information@birdobservers.org.au

For regional Birds Australia groups:
    birdsaustralia.com.au

Quiz / 1. to examine or test informally by questions. 2. now obsolete, an eccentric person.

If you are this far into the book and still not sure whether you are a birder or not, try this simple quiz on page 174 to establish your bird-nerd status.

DIY IDENTIFICATION

BIRD-NERD RATING QUIZ

1 What do you first think of when you hear the words 'a pair of Brown Boobies'?

A: Pamela Anderson in *Baywatch*.

B: A type of tropical seabird.

C: Bird number 423 on my Australian list.

2 Do you own an anorak?

A: No.

B: Yes.

C: Yes. I don't own *an* anorak; I own several, one for each day of the week.

3 How did September 11 change the world for you?

A: It made me feel less safe, and caused me to question our place in the world.

B: It made it impossible to take my spotlight battery on international flights.

C: It delayed my plans to see an Afghanistan Warbler by a few years.

4 What does Werribee Sewage Farm mean to you?

A: The final resting place for what I flush down the loo.

B: A good habitat for waterbirds.

C: The happiest place on Earth.

5 What is your favourite thing to snuggle into bed with at night?

A: A warm, loving partner.

B: Volume 7 of the *Handbook of Australian, New Zealand and Antarctic Birds*.

C: My anorak, so that I don't waste time in the morning and miss precious seconds on deck looking for seabirds to add to my list.

6 Driving at night, you come across a Rufous Owl that has clearly just been hit by a truck. Do you:

A: Stop to check if it is alive, in which case you would take it to a wildlife carer.

B: Stop to check if it is alive, as you don't have Rufous Owl on your list, and dead birds don't count.

C: Stop to check if it is alive, and if not, give it mouth-to-mouth as you really, really need Rufous Owl for your list.

For every time you answered C give yourself 10 points, 5 points for every B and no points for A.

If you heard or saw any birds while doing this quiz, add another 20 points to your score.

If you could identify the birds you heard and saw while doing this quiz, add a further 20 points.

YOUR SCORE:

50–100 points: You definitely are a birdwatcher. In fact, so severe is your habit that you most probably qualify as a twitcher (see TWITCHER). Twitching is such a dangerous and debilitating addiction that it was the one thing Ben Cousins said no to.

10–50 points: You most definitely have strong birdwatching tendencies, though you are not quite as far down the path of no return as the twitcher. With a lot of support from loved ones and professional therapy you may just pull through (see A QUALIFIED MENTAL HEALTH PROFESSIONAL).

0–10 points: Let's face it; you are a dude, Dude. You will never know the joys of wading up to your waist in a stinking sewage pond on a 35-degree day waiting for a Hudsonian Godwit to raise its wings so that you can see the black armpit that distinguishes it from the other thousand otherwise identical-looking godwits it is standing with. You lucky, lucky bastard.

Rarities / what keeps a twitcher going, and truth be known, I reckon every birder enjoys seeing something rare or unusual.

There are different levels of rarity. A Red Wattlebird may be rare for your local patch (*see* LOCAL PATCH) if it has never been seen there before but as they are generally quite a common bird, it would not be a rarity unless you happened to live somewhere like Tasmania or the Northern Territory where Red Wattlebirds are unknown – *then* it would be a rarity.

Similarly, there are probably millions of Rosy Starlings in the world, but as only three have ever made it to Australia they are treated as a royal rarity here, so much so that people will drop everything to get halfway around the country to see one (*see* DIP). There are, on the other hand, dozens of records of Orange-bellied Parrot each year on the mainland in winter; yet in a global context, these are in every sense of the word a rarity, with only around 140 birds in the wild. They are still considered a local rarity too, despite the number of records, because these all come from the same few locations where the parrots are regularly found, and even then they are not guaranteed.

In one sense, a rarity is a bird you haven't seen – once it's on your list, it is no longer anywhere near as rare for you.

But perhaps a better stab at a definition of what constitutes a real rarity is that provided by the Birds Australia Rarities Committee, which requires submissions made for all birds that have been seen less than five times in the last five years. That's pretty rare.

There is no official measure of what a rarity is, though, and so rarity really is in the eye of the beholder. If a Banded Lapwing is rare for you, that's great, because they are a very cool bird; whenever I see one, I get a similar thrill to that which I get when I see a rarity – maybe not quite the same as seeing a Grey-headed Lapwing, a first for Australia that I had deliberately gone to twitch, but a thrill nonetheless.

Rarities committees / the bodies that determine whether a sighting is accepted as an 'official' sighting.

Almost every birder agrees that there needs to be some sort of verification process to accept claims of rare and unusual species. Ultimately birding is about truth – every single species of bird must belong to a species (and we won't even touch on the debate of how to categorise a hybrid) and, in discovering what that species is, the birder is uncovering a little nugget of empirical truth. A repository for all these little nuggets is generally thought to be a good idea. And so the idea of rarities committees, consisting of a group of expert birders to adjudicate on unusual claims, has developed.

There are several state-based rarities committees who deal with sightings of birds rare for that state. The only truly national body is the Birds Australia Rarities Committee (BARC), which supposedly gives the nod as to whether new sightings are added to the official Australian list.

The trouble with rarities committees such as BARC is that they have to judge the likelihood of birders' claims, and human nature being what it is, people don't like rejection in any form. It is very hard to separate a judgment of your claim from a judgment of you. I have heard of birders complaining that in having had their claims rejected they feel as though they have been branded a liar, and hence they will never submit further sightings.

This attitude means that BARC and similar committees end up failing to fulfil their function adequately, as many records are never submitted; thereby we end up with an incomplete picture of the state of play within Australia's birding scene.

So in an effort to encourage everybody that sees a vagrant species to submit to BARC (or any appropriate rarities committee), I offer these tips on getting your submission accepted (*see* VAGRANT). Not that I speak with enormous authority on the matter, for while I have never had a BARC submission rejected, that is because I have never actually submitted one myself. Until the last couple of years I had never seen anything significant enough to warrant a BARC submission, but now that I have (*see* FIRSTS), let me assure you that I fully intend to . . . one day.

In fact, it is through talking with various past and present members about what they would require for my submission that I picked up these tips that I am passing on. It is not a cheat sheet as such, but more of a style guide that might help get your submission accepted, because often it is the way the submission is written that sees it go down in flames.

1. Make sure you write a decent description

Sometimes it doesn't even have to be particularly detailed, it just has to be more than 'I saw an Abbott's Booby [that's a Christmas Island endemic seabird, not one of the Federal Health Minister's latest political gaffes] in downtown

Broken Hill the other day'. Amazingly, descriptions come in that don't even mention what family the bird belonged to – it is assumed that because the species name is up the top of the submission there is no need to elaborate, but the committee need to know that you know why it was a booby and not a tern or a pelican or something even more bizarre.

Simply writing 'it had black wings and a white back' without any reference to size or shape or any other features helps no one. You could as easily be describing a magpie as an Abbott's Booby.

2. Don't transpose somebody else's description

It is amazing how often rarities committees get a description of a bird lifted word for word from a field guide. It certainly doesn't inspire confidence that the observer has independently thought about why the bird was what is claimed. All it shows is that they have read that particular field guide. If anything, pointing out how your bird was different to the field guide can create a more convincing argument if you can justify it: 'though this bird had a relatively stubby bill, which would suggest a Semi-palmated Plover, other diagnostic features noted such as call, lack of palmations on the feet and the shape of the breast band clearly indicate it was a Ringed Plover.' A statement such as this clearly demonstrates that you know what to look for.

And remember; field guides aren't infallible. So the segment you may be quoting may actually be incorrect. And whatever you do, never, ever talk about the red spot on a Horsfield's Bronze-Cuckoo (*see* FIELD GUIDES)!

3. Tell them what it wasn't, as much as what it was

Many a submission fails, not because the committee thinks it wasn't what the observer says it was, but because other likely species were not ruled out. There have been many more Ringed Plovers in Australia than have been accepted by BARC simply because many of the submissions have not ruled out the very similar Semi-palmated Plover. Perhaps BARC are on the overly cautious side, but I suspect that is a better approach than the other, which would let a few rough-around-the-edges, if not downright dodgy, claims slide through. This way, if a record gets through the committee, you can be certain the case was airtight.

4. Don't make it personal

Even BARC members themselves have their records rejected by BARC, so it is not – as some like to think – a personal vendetta against a birder when a record is rejected. (Birders are great conspiracy theorists.) But so many submissions make it personal, because their prime justification for why they are claiming a Red-tailed Black-Cockatoo from Canberra (this wouldn't be a BARC submission as it is more of a local rarity), is not a description of the bird in question, but a simple statement that 'I am familiar with this species'. With no other supporting evidence, the submitter of such a record is putting themselves forward as the sole reason why the sighting should be believed, and as with credit, 'refusal can offend'.

5. Submit supporting material

In the case of rarities submissions, a picture really does say a thousand words. But copies of original notes and sketches or corroborating testimony from other observers all makes it that much easier for the committee to accept your record, because, believe it or not, in most instances that is what they are trying to do.

Of course, I reserve judgment on all of this until after I see whether my Middendorff's Grasshopper-Warbler gets through (*see* FIRSTS). Because if it doesn't …

ACTION: Before submitting a rare sighting record, check out BARC's website at
users.bigpond.net.au/palliser/barc/barc-home.html
As well as contact details, it has previous case reviews and a list of species that they require submissions for. It will give you a far better idea of what they look for and how to go about submitting.

Ravens / moderately large black birds that, along with the crows, are members of the corvid family.

There are three species of raven in Australia and they are all, within their range, quite common. But talk to any non-birdwatcher and they will tell you every time that they are crows. And no amount of reasoning or showing them the maps in your bird book or your PhD in applied ornithology will persuade them otherwise. I firmly believe that the legal defense of provocation to murder should be denied in all but one circumstance: where a non-birder tries to tell a birder that a particular black bird is a crow.

Identifying corvid species is no easy task – in Australia their identity wasn't properly sorted out until the late 1960s. But the non-expert always has some tin-pot theory on how to tell a crow from a raven, no matter how wrong it is. The simple fact is that the only difference in this country between ravens and crows is that ravens have brownish-grey

> **For the record, here is a guide to the dominant corvid in each Australian capital city**
>
> Adelaide: Little Raven
>
> Brisbane: Torresian Crow
>
> Canberra: Australian Raven
>
> Darwin: Torresian Crow
>
> Hobart: Forest Raven
>
> Melbourne: Little Raven
>
> Perth: Australian Raven
>
> Sydney: Australian Raven

down at the base of their feathers and crows have white down at the base of their feathers – a feature that can only be seen in a howling gale.

But virtually any non-birder in each of these cities will tell you they are seeing crows, and what's more, that they'd know the difference. Only in the New England area of New South Wales where all five Australian corvids have been found is there legitimate reason for general confusion, and the same is true to a lesser extent in the outback, where a corvid could be either an Australian Raven or the widespread arid species, the Little Crow. But it isn't the people in the outback making the erroneous statements, it is usually those who live over 500 kilometres away from the nearest possible crow that continue to get it wrong.

A Melbourne radio station once rang me live on air to settle the dispute for them. I was introduced as a leading bird expert, which was a bit of a stretch, but the audience wasn't to know that. I gave them the unequivocal statement on how to tell a raven from a crow and was so adamant, forceful and humourless about it that I thought it was clear that, apart from a few near Mildura, there are no crows in Victoria.

The very next caller rang in and said, 'What that bird fella said is all well and good, but where we live, we get the crows coming down from the mountains before a big storm.' I rang back the radio station asking for the caller's name and address, but once they had established that I was intending to run him down dressed in a raven outfit, they declined to pass the details on.

Red-necked Phalarope / a small wader that breeds in the Arctic and winters generally at sea in tropical regions, rarely making it as far as Australia.

To my mind, the first Australian sighting of a Red-necked Phalarope at Werribee Sewage Farm by two observers on 22 December 1962 signals the dawning of the modern era of Australian birdwatching. In order to identify the phalarope, the observers would have had to take an international perspective, as it certainly wouldn't have been in any Australian bird books. This was a threshold bird, and within the next decade, a whole swag of new birds for Australia would be found.

More and more birders started to get out there actively looking for rarities; hence, the Australian list, which had been essentially static for many years, began to rise.

The fact that since 1962 there have been dozens of records of Red-necked Phalarope from across the country (they even occur annually in small flocks at the Port Hedland Saltworks) suggests that they had almost certainly occurred in Australia before 1962. It was just that nobody was really looking for them, or had the requisite skills to identify them. Today there are still probably hundreds of vagrants missed every year, across the enormous sweep of the country, but with more people out there looking it is inevitable that fewer will go undetected.

Reverse migration / like overshooting, reverse migration is a method whereby a vagrant makes it to Australia when it should, by rights, be somewhere overseas.

Though it may have simply overshot, it is probable that the Grey-headed Lapwing (*see* GREY-HEADED LAPWING) was a reverse migrant, judging by the dates it was seen. First sighted in June 2006 (though it could well have been here for months or years before then) it seemed to have disappeared by late October. The fact that the bird appeared to be in breeding plumage, which it would be at that time of year if it was where it was supposed to be, only adds to the reverse migration theory.

What possibly happened is that this individual, like the rest of its species, moved from its summer breeding grounds in China and Japan to the usual winter haunts stretching from Hong Kong to Kolkutta. Come the northern spring (March–April) the birds would have all headed north, but something went wrong with this individual's internal compass and it went south instead.

Twitchers have their own reverse migration, for when everybody is abandoning the far north of the country in the steamy wet season, twitchers' eyes turn to the possibility of vagrants turning up there, blown in by a cyclone or two. Similarly in winter, when most sensible folk are heading north to follow the sun, a twitcher's thoughts turn to the Southern Ocean; the stormier the better, for this is the weather that brings rare Southern Ocean seabirds close in to shore (*see* MOULT, OVERSHOOTING, SEA WATCHING).

Rime of the Ancient Mariner / poem by Samuel Taylor Coleridge that gave us the classic lines 'Water, water everywhere and not a drop to drink' and 'All things both great and small'.

Coleridge also gave us the concept of an albatross around one's neck, referring to the albatross that the said mariner kills, bringing bad luck to him and all those aboard his ship. As canonical as this piece is in world literature, the question remains for the twitcher, 'What kind of albatross was it?'

Most assume that the poem refers to the Wandering Albatross, one of the largest and best-known of the family, partly because when the bird first approaches, the mariner's ship is so far south that 'The ice was here, the ice was there, the ice was all around'. But in such truly Antarctic seas at least five species of albatross could be expected. As there are no actual descriptions of plumage in the poem, the bird's identity will probably always remain unknown – a salutary lesson in the need for comprehensive field notes.

As it turns out, Coleridge was inspired by an actual account of a sailor killing an albatross, according to Coleridge's mate William Wordsworth (who, incidentally, writing from England, sadly had to content himself with producing poems about such dull birds as the Skylark. Skylark? What a yawn. If he were an Aussie, now, he would have had a far greater selection of interesting birds to write about). Wordsworth records that, in the original story, the sailor killed a black albatross somewhere off the west coast of the Americas.

This may have referred to a juvenile Wandering Albatross, though these young birds aren't really black, more of a milk-chocolate colour, so it is possible the prototype for the poem could have been either a Sooty Albatross, Black-footed Albatross or the juvenile Short-tailed Albatross, all of which are blacker than the juvenile Wanderer. Then again, the original sailor may have completely misidentified a giant petrel, which approaches an albatross in size. But whereas the albatross is all grace and ethereal beauty, the giant petrel is the bovver boy of the ocean – a thuggish, hump-backed pirate that gets its food by eating carrion or forcing other seabirds to give up their catch. How ironic if the mariner suffered all manner of agony for killing a bird that only a mother could love.

Rufous Scrub-bird / one of only two scrub-bird species, its only other relative being the lyrebirds although it is nowhere near as spectacular and showy; one of the biggest buggers of a bird to find in Australia.

Rules of twitching / the rules that determine what birds can and can't be included on your list.

These days, this bird is generally confined to a few mountain tops along the east coast that are dominated by ancient Antarctic Beech forests. There are virtually no easy access points to Rufous Scrub-bird habitat and even when you have walked in, they are exceptionally difficult to see because they rarely raise their head above the ground cover they feed on. There are reports of scrub-birds even scurrying rodent-style under leaf litter. This was quite a bogey bird for me but after many attempts I eventually saw the bird by crawling along the dank rainforest floor for half an hour (*see* BOGEY BIRD). Sometimes birding can be such fun!

1. **A bird can only be counted for your list if it is free-flying and in the wild.**
   This means that dead birds can't be counted. Neither can birds seen in zoos, on television or in your dreams. Eggs don't count either, not until they've hatched. Nor do kids on a work-for-the-dole scheme who are forced to dress up in chicken costumes and stand on the street advertising car yards.

2. A bird must be seen within a prescribed territory.

For the Australian checklist, this includes all of Australia and all offshore territories (excluding Antarctica, presumably because its legal status as an Australian territory is disputed) and out to the 200–nautical-mile limit. For each state, it is within the borders of that state, and supposedly only out to the 3-nautical-mile limit (where the jurisdiction of the state is said to end) though hardly anyone I know seems to adhere to that rule.

If you were on the border of South Australia and New South Wales and saw an Eyrean Grasswren in South Australia from the New South Wales side of the border, you could not count it for your New South Wales list. Which would be a major downer as there are no records of Eyrean Grasswren from New South Wales. It would certainly have you thinking about jumping the border fence and trying to flush it across (*see* FLUSH), but that of course would be unethical (*see* ETHICAL BIRDWATCHING).

3. A bird may only be counted in accordance with the official checklist.

It's a contentious issue as to which checklist should be deemed official, but the majority of birders opt to follow Birds Australia's 1994 checklist by Christidis and Boles (*see* CHECKLIST).

If you see a bird that is not on the checklist, technically you shouldn't be able to tick it until that sighting has been approved by BARC (*see* RARITIES COMMITTEES). Since 1994 a couple of dozen birds have been added to the list in such a manner. You could include a bird on your list that has either not been submitted to BARC or has been rejected by it, but then you are not singing from the same songbook, so there is little point comparing your list against those of other twitchers. And it doesn't bode well for your reputation if you continue to claim that Night Parrot that everybody else believed was nothing more than a fat budgie.

4. A bird must be seen well enough to establish its identity.

This may seem self-evident but it is surprising how often this rule gets stretched. I believe that you should be very strict in what constitutes a tickable view because, in the end, the only person you are really cheating is yourself. I can't see how there can be any satisfaction in adding a bird to your list if you haven't really experienced the full essence of the bird. But it does become tempting to tick off a bird on poor views, particularly when you know that what you saw just had to be that species, or when other birders with you saw the bird better than you did. As painful as it can be to leave that Antarctic Prion box unticked on your life list, it is so much more satisfying when you actually see the bird properly. If you really want to tick it, why not start a list entitled, 'Birds that Kevin saw in my presence that I dipped out on'.

In the end though, what you count on your own list is entirely up to you. These are not life-and-death matters, despite the seriousness with which they are treated by some. And, as astonishing as it may seem, some people don't even keep a list, and they continue to birdwatch happily without one. Amazing but true.

Seabirders / birdwatchers whose idea of fun is to go out onto the ocean in tiny little fishing boats, to spend long hours being thrown about on the waves, to get covered in spray as they chuck fish guts overboard to a bunch of hungry sea birds and to pay substantial sums of money for the privilege! Idiots, in other words.

The seabirders' motto is 'Seabirders are Real Birders', which is an acknowledgment of the difficulties of birding at sea (*see* PELAGIC). You are bouncing around and the birds are wheeling past at speed, disappearing behind waves. Just to get your bins on one is a feat in itself. And the birds themselves can be very tricky to identify; often it comes down to the extent of black in the undertail. No wonder seabirders have a strong streak of arrogance about them; they walk with the same kind of misguided cocky swagger you see in a mountain climber or free base cliff-jumper – that 'I do something really out there' kind of attitude. I say 'misguided' because, buddy, nobody else actually wants to do it.

Seasickness / what you will most likely experience if you want to see the majority of the 70-plus species of seabirds found in Australian waters (*see* PELAGIC).

I have seen birders be sick within the first half hour of a boat trip even after taking their seasickness medication. As these expeditions tend to be for a minimum of eight hours these victims face a living hell, becoming so stricken that they are incapable of even raising their binoculars.

There are as many seasickness remedies as there are birders who have gone out to sea, and in many cases they will directly contradict each other. Some swear by ginger tablets, which have none of the side effects of pharmaceutical cures, but I stick with my medication because I have never actually been sick on them (though I have come close) and I figure, 'Why jump off a winning horse?'

So for what it is worth, here are my tips on how to make pelagics as pleasant as possible. This is merely what works for me; there is no guarantee of effectiveness for anyone else.

Usually pelagics start very early when you don't much feel like eating, but I always try to have a light breakfast to line my stomach, unlike some who refuse to eat anything even the night before. I figure that at least I won't be losing my stomach lining the very first time I chuck. I find toast is good, or cereal, though a hearty feast of greasy bacon and eggs may be tempting fate a little too much. I even drink orange juice, which makes certain people recoil in horror, but I have never found that citrus upsets my stomach. If it does for you, then perhaps avoid this.

On the subject of drinks, a sensible idea is to avoid alcohol the night before, though I have to say that some of the best sailors I know are also some of the best drinkers. Perhaps they are so accustomed to being unsteady on their feet that being thrown off balance in a five-metre swell is like a walk (home) in the park. I tend to avoid alcohol the night before, as it seems to interfere with my seasickness medication. One tip is to take one tablet before going to sleep the night before and another half an hour before getting on the boat. If anything, it means you get a good night's sleep as most medications have a sedative effect. But even just one or two beers can reverse this effect and cause me to spend the night before staring at the ceiling, unable to sleep and getting more anxious because of it.

I always stay out in the fresh air, no matter how wet or cold I get. The cabin of the boat may be warm and dry but it is also invariably stuffy, smelly and has me wanting to heave within seconds. When on deck, I try and position myself as close to the rear as possible. It usually rocks less at the stern, and you tend to get a more uninterrupted view of the open ocean in which to scan for birds. The downside is that you may get a faceful of diesel exhaust fumes and, if it is a small boat, the spray from the bow in rough weather will come crashing down on you, not to mention the vomit from seasick passengers on the upper deck (*see* PARABOLIC GROT).

On board I try to eat snacks at regular intervals. Chewing helps to dissipate tension building in the stomach, as does burping and yawning. Snacks that I like to stuff into my pockets (so I don't have to go inside the cabin) include: apples, muesli bars and biscuits. Chewy mints are good value, not least because they make your burps seem refreshing and not vomitous.

I agree with the theory that it is best to look out to the horizon, so I try to avoid taking notes, reading or fiddling about with photographic equipment, particularly viewfinders.

The best cure for seasickness is to have an exciting trip. The rush of adrenaline involved in seeing a new or rare bird is usually enough to overcome any welling nausea. Sadly, after your first pelagic trip, days at sea consist of about 90 per cent tedium with a few flashes of excitement.

I find singing songs quietly under my breath to be quite soothing. For some reason The Beatles' 'In My Life' is the most calming of all. It is best not to let anyone see your lips moving as they may think it is an indication that you are up for a chat. I firmly believe it best to avoid excessive conversation. Trying to be heard above the throb of the diesel engines places extra strain on already tense stomach muscles, and there is every chance you will get stuck next to an interminable bore, thereby raising the tedium score from 90 to 99 per cent.

 ACTION: If you find yourself wedged next to a chatterbox who takes your Easter Island facade as an invitation for a chinwag, explain politely but firmly that you are feeling a bit green and need to conserve your energies. If that doesn't work, try actually throwing up on them. People say you often feel much better once you have chucked your guts up, so heaving all over your assailant rather than over the side can only make you feel twice as good.

Sea watching / trekking out to an exposed spot on the coast, preferably a high promontory or cape that juts out into the surrounding sea, and sitting for hours as you scan the oceans for any birds that fly past; the worse the weather the better, as deep ocean species are more likely to be blown towards shore.

As you can imagine, sea watching has never been very popular, and it's even less so now that pelagics are more common. Nowadays, if you want to tick off a White-chinned Petrel you can take a pelagic off the southern coast in winter and have one come within touching distance at the back of the boat, as opposed to spending hours shivering, sitting on the cold, wet ground and seeing a distant speck several miles away on the horizon that just might be a White-chinned Petrel – or possibly a Great-winged Petrel, or a Short-tailed Shearwater, or a speck of dirt on the end of your telescope.

These days it seems the only regular sea watches are held off Sydney, with Magic Point near Maroubra being a favoured site, though any of the headlands on the city's coast can be fruitful. One birder has managed to snare himself an apartment looking out to sea and has set up a telescope where he can sea watch from the privacy of his lounge room. Apparently he has got a house list to die for.

Other traditionally good sites to go for sea watching are:

Queensland: Point Lookout on North Stradbroke Island

New South Wales: Green Cape, near Eden, Norah Head on the Central Coast

Victoria: Cape Schanck, Point Lonsdale, Cape Nelson, near Portland

Tasmania: Tasman's Arch, Cape Toureville on the east coast, and almost any prominent headland on the west coast

South Australia: Newland Head (or, as access is now rather difficult, try nearby Parson's Head)

Western Australia: the Gap near Albany, Cape Leeuwin

700 Club / 1. a conservative Christian cable TV show in America, the membership of which consists chiefly of zealous fanatics. **2.** an unofficial club for birdwatchers who have seen 700 or more species of bird in Australia, membership of which consists chiefly of zealous fanatics.

The 700 Club used to be very exclusive. It wasn't until the late 1970s that the first twitchers even qualified for membership of the 600 club, and by the start of the 1990s only one or two had reached 700. In 2006 the club welcomed its fiftieth member. Currently the leading twitcher has a list of 792, and if he can keep going he will become the first member of the 800 club, an idea that even as recently as twenty years ago would have seemed as remote as space travel to the Wright Brothers.

One of the great myths of birdwatching is that in order to be a member of the 700 Club one must be an exceptionally good birdwatcher. While undoubtedly a large percentage of the 50 club members are top-notch birders, there is the occasional duffer amongst this elite. I mean, I've seen over 700 myself, so what does that say? Being good at identifying birds is of minor importance when compared to the two main preconditions to entry: having plenty of money and time.

To see 700 birds in Australia, you either have to be quite well-off, or if not, prepared to sacrifice a large slice of your income to chasing after rare birds. Even just to see all the resident species is a mammoth task as every bird has a particular habitat preference and some of these habitats are very far flung indeed. Thus even to see a majority of the 730-odd birds that regularly call Australia home, one needs to travel vast distances – to Cape York Peninsula for Golden-shouldered Parrot, down to Tassie for Dusky Robin, over to south-western Australia for Red-eared Firetail and out into the sandy deserts for Eyrean Grasswren. And that's even before you head off to the external territories such as Christmas Island for the Christmas Island Imperial-Pigeon and Heard Island for Black-faced Sheathbill, or go out to sea on numerous pelagic trips to look for 70-odd species of seabird such as Buller's Shearwater off the New South Wales coast, and Matsudaira's Storm-Petrel out from Broome. As you are very unlikely to see all your target species in the one trip, you can fork out enormous sums in the quest for 700.

Of course, the longer you have been in the game the greater the likelihood of getting some top birds on your list that the newer twitchers will struggle to unblock (*see* BLOCKERS). For instance, there haven't been sightings of some birds such as Wilson's Phalarope or White-rumped Sandpiper since the 1980s, so anyone who started twitching since then is at least two behind the older brigade. As I was too young to drive then, I knew about these rarities but never got to see them, so I feel doubly gripped off (*see* GRIPPING OFF). But as one idiot proved in 2002, it is possible to get your 700 in as short a period as a year. Travelling to all points except the sub-Antarctic Macquarie and Heard Islands and Ashmore Reef in the north, I just managed to scrape past 700 in my Big Twitch year. Though I was fortunate to have chosen an exceptional year for vagrants to turn up, I did nothing but birdwatch for the entire year, cramming what would be about ten years of serious birding (based on two or three serious birding trips a year) into twelve months. But that was when I was in a serious Captain Twitchpants phase (*see* CAPTAIN TWITCHPANTS). I'm much better now . . . honest.

Shakespeare / an English writer, pretty handy when it came to encapsulating the human condition, and who, as it turns out, knew a thing or two about birds.

Ever since the earliest scribes took up the first chisel and cuneiform tablets, they have been writing about birds, I guess because they are one of the most obvious and visible members of the animal kingdom, coupled with the mystery and magic of flight. It is no surprise, therefore, that birds feature often in the works of Shakespeare, from the hoarse raven that welcomes King Duncan under Lady Macbeth's battlements to Hamlet declaring that he was only selectively mad, as he could still tell a hawk from a handsaw (a handsaw being a corruption of the word for a young heron, hernshaw, so he meant that he was sane enough to tell the hunter from its prey).

From an identification point of view, however, Shakespeare may not be all that reliable. The hawk that Hamlet talks about is likely to be one of four species – the Hobby, Kestrel, Merlin and Sparrowhawk – none of which realistically approaches the size to take on even a young heron. Not that I am saying Shakespeare was a stringer (*see* STRINGER), just that more likely he meant one of the larger birds of prey, like an eagle or even a buzzard, but the lure of alliteration was too great.

So as a modern birder I wouldn't be looking to *The Merchant of Venice* or *Coriolanus* for inspiration, though there are a couple of areas where Shakespeare is still of relevance. Firstly, Shakespeare does signal some of the ecological changes that have occurred since the end of the sixteenth century. King Lear, when betrayed by his daughter Goneril, venomously calls her 'detested kite'. The kite would have been familiar to Londoners as a scavenger on the rubbish heaps around town. Though the birds would have been doing the townsfolk a favour by removing carrion and other dead matter, they were reviled as evil, opportunistic birds. What is interesting is that this species, the Red Kite, had by the twentieth century been long gone from London, and, apart from a few in the highlands of Central Wales, was found nowhere else in Britain. It is currently the subject of a concerted reintroduction program.

Similarly, later in the play, Edgar as 'Poor Tom' tries to convince a blinded Gloucester that they are above the cliffs at Dover, referring to the choughs flying halfway down the cliffs. In Shakespeare's time, the chough, a bird favouring sea cliffs, would have been present at Dover. They are not there today, nor have they been for centuries. Thus Shakespeare chronicles the decline of the chough.

But the real significance of Shakespeare to the modern birder is that, as far as I am aware, he records the first instance of an argument over bird identification. It occurs the morning after Romeo and Juliet have been secretly married. Romeo has to flee to Mantua or face certain death at the hand of Juliet's father and, as the dawn approaches, they argue over whether the bird they hear is the night-singing nightingale or the harbinger of the morning, the lark. If only the modern field guide had been around, they would have saved themselves an awful lot of trouble. I imagine the scene would have then gone something like this . . .

JULIET
Wilt thou be gone? It is not yet near day.
It was the nightingale, and not the lark,
That pierced the fearful hollow of thine ear.

ROMEO
It was the lark, the herald of the morn:
No nightingale.

JULIET
Believe me, love, it was the nightingale.

ROMEO
Thou art mistaken, my sweet,
For Jonsson's *Birds of Europe* clearly asserts,
The song of the nightingale 'contains clear,
Indrawn whistles, "tinny" fluted "jook" notes,
And rattling sequences', oft repeated.
Whereas yon songster warbling,
Is possessed more of the 'variable,
'Chrriup', 'trruwee' character of the lark.

JULIET
It is, it is! Hie hence, be gone, away!
It is the lark that sings so out of tune.

And in true twitcher fashion, upon hearing a new bird, Romeo dashes out into the fields to look for it.

Of course, if Romeo and Juliet had been true twitchers they would have been asking themselves what species of lark they were dealing with. A Skylark? A Crested Lark? A Bimaculated, Short-toed or Lesser Short-toed Lark? Just exactly what kind of lark are we talking about here?

Ship-assisted vagrants / birds that arrive on our shores by boat.

It's not just groups of leering bogans with a penchant for partying and a pocketful of date-rape drugs that appreciate our modern ocean-going transport; lured by the chance of a free feed and a convenient resting place, many birds have found ways to make use of it as well.

For centuries seabirds have been following fishing vessels to feed from the by-catch thrown overboard by the fishermen, though of recent times this habit has been at their own peril (*see* ALBATROSS). Oceanic islands that have never been part of a mainland, such as Lord Howe and Christmas Island, have populations of small, non-sea-going birds, which suggests that these birds must have got there under their own steam. On a ferry trip from Malaita to Guadalcanal in the Solomon Islands, I noticed that every single floating coconut had a tern or a booby (*see* UNCLE TREVOR) perched upon it. There is no reason why a small bird wouldn't do the same if it found itself blown out to sea. To a bird, the difference between a coconut, a floating log and a ship is negligible – they provide a place of rest on which not to drown.

And yet, unlike many other birding jurisdictions which recognise the opportunism of wild birds, Australia's rule is that if a bird arrives in the country on a vessel, it cannot be counted. Its assisted passage means it is untickable, unless it somehow manages to find a mate, breed and establish a viable population that lasts for more than ten years.

I have no problem applying this rule to birds that clearly would be incapable of arriving on our shores without direct human aid (like the Black-billed Magpie, a known weak flyer that is regularly kept in cages that miraculously turned up in Newcastle, New South Wales, a mighty long way from its Eurasian home), but for notorious stowaways such as House Crow I think they should be tickable; especially when birds such as Franklin's and Laughing Gulls are on the Australian list. Both these birds breed on the prairies of North America and migrate to South America for the winter. In most cases where they have turned up in Australia, it has been within cooee of an international port. You can't tell me these birds didn't hitch a free ride across the Pacific – and yet, because they are gulls, they are deemed to count.

You see, this is the sort of crap that gets a twitcher fired up – not global warming or the appalling loss of habitat worldwide, but whether a gull that has been ship-assisted can be included on the twitcher's list. It's pathetic really. But dammit, I've seen House Crow twice now and I want it on my list. Any political party that puts that on its platform will get my vote!

 ACTION: If you really want to add a new species to the Australian list, buy a large boat, and sail across to Asia. Load up the deck with all types of food that Asian birds love and hope that they are attracted to it long enough for you to sail into Australian waters. Better still, if you want to add a new family to the Australian list, plant an old-growth forest on deck to encourage woodpeckers of hornbills – you'd be the most popular twitcher in the history of the sport.

South Australia / a large, predominantly arid state; hence the bulk of the human population crowds into the relatively fertile south-eastern corner; the only colony not to take convicts – a huge mistake, because everybody knows that villains are far more cool and interesting than goody-goodies, and South Australians have thereafter had to struggle to convince the rest of the country that the place isn't entirely boring.

South Australia is the crossroads state. Many eastern species reach the western limit of their range here and some western specialties are found no further east. As a result it tends to be somewhat overlooked by birders, as they can more easily find such species elsewhere, along with many others that don't make it into South Australia; a feeling compounded by the fact that the state has only one endemic species, Chestnut-breasted Whiteface. This is a pity as it has a list of almost 470 species, many of which are highly sought-after birds, and yields some of the greatest desert birding in the country. Birds of the calibre of Thick-billed, Grey and Eyrean Grasswrens, Inland Dotterel, Black-eared Miner and Scarlet-chested Parrot are all very gettable in South Australia.

The best inland areas are along the Strzelecki and Birdsville Tracks, and Gluepot Reserve in the Murray Mallee. Along the coast there are some brilliant sites, including Kangaroo Island, and the Penrice Saltfields just north of Adelaide is one of the top wader sites in the country.

South Australians tend to be a fiercely parochial lot, and like to do things their own way. Not surprisingly then, the national birding groups are poorly represented in South Australia, where the main bird organisation (and the first established in this country, in 1899) is the South Australian Ornithological Association (SAOA), which in recent years, like the RAOU, has adopted a more manageable name in Birds SA. South Australians are often associated with crows, not because of the number of crows there, but because they can't help crowing about even their slightest achievement. Hence one of my greatest birding goals is to find a Chestnut-breasted Whiteface just across the border in the Northern Territory, just so I can see the look on the South Australians' faces as they lose their only endemic bird.

ACTION: Birds SA can be contacted at:
c/- South Australian Museum,
North Terrace,
Adelaide,
South Australia, 5000
www.birdssa.asn.au

Species / the biological unit of classification most often used by birders when compiling their lists.

Oh, if only it were that simple.

What does and doesn't constitute a full species inflames passions like virtually nothing else in the birding world. In Australia the argument flares mostly over albatross taxonomy, with one camp claiming there are 24 species of albatross in the world (20 of which have occurred in Australian waters) while the other maintains there are only 14 (ten in Australia) (*see* TAXONOMY). Then there is the rest of the birding community, left scratching their heads wondering what the hell the two opposing camps are going on about. Well, hold onto your hats, people, 'cause I'm going in . . .

Until recently the prevailing scientific orthodoxy held that a species was a unique population that, in normal circumstances, solely bred with members of that same population. This is known as the biological species concept (BSC). Smaller subsets of a population, called sub-species or races (which as far as I can ascertain are basically the same thing) though sometimes looking quite different, would still readily interbreed with other races of the same species, especially where the range of two races overlapped. This meant there was a zone of integration where the characteristics of both forms would merge.

Speciation normally occurs when populations have been separated and they follow different evolutionary paths, responding to the different conditions in their respective environments. But as any aviculturalist with a bit of a Frankenstein bent can tell you, birds are randy little buggers and will attempt to mate with almost anything, and you can get hybrids of pretty much any two species in the same family if you get them together long enough and ply them with a few drinks and a little Barry White music. But this doesn't mean they should be considered the same species.

As we have altered and fragmented natural ecosystems, species that were quite happily evolving down separate paths have now come into contact in a way that wouldn't naturally have occurred. Thus the Yellow-throated Miner, a bird of more open country, was able to move in on its Black-eared Miner cousin's home turf of dense mallee woodlands, once the farmers came in with their stump-jump ploughs and cleared the land. The more numerous Yellow-throated Miner began to mate up with some Black-eareds and genetically swamp them, so pure-bred birds became very rare indeed. A strict adherence to the BSC would say that they were no longer distinct species because they were now interbreeding, which seemed to many to be clearly wrong.

In part to deal with problems such as this, a new approach was developed, the Phylogenetic Species Concept (PSC), which defined a species as the smallest possible unit of a population that was distinct. It is essentially taking a smaller standard unit as the benchmark for a species than the BSC does. Thus all previous races and sub-species would be accorded full species status, and with the advent of DNA technology proving that even identical-looking species have populations that are genetically distinct within them, these were likewise to be recognised as full species.

Adopting the PSC wholesale would virtually double the number of bird species overnight. You would think that tick-hungry birders would welcome the chance of a plethora of armchair ticks. But the PSC throws up certain problems. If it is impossible to identify a species by sight, then where's the fun in going birding? Taken to its logical ends, the PSC would be highly unmanageable; any little difference could throw up a new species, and what constitutes a hybrid would remain quite unclear.

This sounds like an esoteric matter that need concern no one bar a few nerdy scientists, but it does have practical implications that can directly impact on birds, especially on bird conservation.

For some reason, governments and the public in general place a greater importance on conserving a species. They are less likely to make an effort to save something that is merely a race of something when other members of the species exist elsewhere. Some journalists tried to stir the pot with this argument over the campaign to save 'Karak', the mascot of the 2006 Commonwealth Games. Karak is actually the endangered race *graptogyne* of the Red-tailed Black-Cockatoo, which is found in south-west Victoria and south-eastern South Australia. When it was pointed out that these birds weren't a distinct species, there was some disquiet, with people feeling they were being ripped off and that the conservation effort was being wasted on a bird that wasn't really rare. But the fact is that this race is distinct and isolated (there won't be any nearby Red-tailed Black-Cockatoos to replace them when they are gone) and to lose them would be as big a tragedy as if they were a full species. So perhaps a PSC approach is more beneficial for conservation outcomes, regardless of its scientific merit.

But there can be a downside in conservation terms with the PSC, especially if it is taken to extremes, and many so-called species are only distinguishable in lab conditions with a slice of DNA. For if we can't tell one species from another, how do we know when we are recording the rarer one? A PSC approach could lead to a dropping off in the reporting rates of some species, because while twitchers will welcome new birds to tick off on their lists, if they are unable to discern what the birds are, the impetus for recording will decline.

There is at least one other philosophical argument pointed out to me by a committed conspiracy theorist, and that is that the PSC inadvertently aids the creationist view of the universe. By taking the smallest end point of difference in a population as defining a species, then the creationist can argue by extension that there is no such thing as evolution; the intelligent designer put all these creatures here, locked in as a species, just as they are. The BSC implicitly acknowledges the evolutionary process, but by a small leap in logic, the PSC could be used to deny it. It wouldn't be the most spurious argument the creationists have put out there.

There is still a long way to go before the BSC/PSC debate is settled. In the meantime, fights will continue to erupt on board pelagics when someone sees a Wandering Albatross and calls it an Antipodean or Gibson's Albatross.

Sport / defined in the *Australian Concise Oxford Dictionary* as 'a game or competitive activity, especially an outdoor one involving physical exertion'. Sounds like birdwatching to me.

Twitching, at any rate, ticks all those boxes. While some may claim it is too serious to be considered a game, it is undoubtedly an extremely competitive activity and the outdoors is essential for play to proceed. As to physicality, try telling a bunch of twitchers that there is no physical exertion involved as they haul themselves up a Northern Territory escarpment for the third sweltering morning in a row in an attempt to nail the White-throated Grasswren.

Make no mistake, twitching is a sport that requires the stamina of an ultra-marathon runner, the driving skills of a rally driver, the precision eyesight of an archer, the navigational ability of an orienteerer, and the rat cunning of a wrestler in a cage match.

Spotless Crake / a small waterbird related to swamphens, this bird does indeed have no spots on its plumage. But it really got its name from the fact that it is so furtive in its habits that of all the crakes it is the hardest to spot.

You hear Spotless Crakes often enough; their common call is a machine-gun staccato that sounds like a little motorbike being started, but preferring to live in the densest of reed beds, they are bloody hard to see.

 ACTION: Often your best chance of seeing a Spotless Crake is at tiny little wetlands, in the suburbs, where they have less habitat to hide in and you are able to have a view of all the muddy edges of the wetlands at once, so that if they come out into the open, as they sometimes do, you will be able to see them.

Spotlighting / the art of finding birds at night with the aid of a torch.

Often the simplest way to see a night bird such as an owl is to find where it roosts during the day (though some species such as Sooty and Masked Owls mainly roost in tree hollows or caves and are rarely seen out in the day). This is not so easy. But even when you have very specific information about a roost site, finding the bird can involve a lot of searching through the foliage and the risk of birder's whiplash from constantly looking up. A far more exciting way to see owls and their mates, though, is at night when they are active.

For this you will need a spotlight. A household torch is usually too weak to be of much use, but going to the other extreme and buying the sort of mega searchlight the Nazis used in *The Great Escape* is liable to burn out the retinas of any poor bird you happen to shine it on. I bought my first spotlight at a gun shop in Griffith, central New South Wales, where the proprietor had great difficulty coming to terms with the fact that I wasn't going to mount the spot on the back of my ute for roo-shooting trips. Even though I explained several times I needed it for birdwatching, not bird-shooting, the model he eventually sold me came with the winking assurance that though powerful, it was so light that it could still be used while holding a shotgun. The first bird I saw with it was a Barn Owl at Hattah-Kulkyne National Park. The beam was so piercing that it literally knocked the startled bird off its perch in shock.

There are all sorts of theories as to what conditions are best for spotlighting, and, in particular, how important moonlight is. The scientific data I have read says the moon makes a minimal difference at best, and varies with the species – some are more active on nights of a bright full moon, others less so. The one constant is that you are going to have far less chance of success on very windy and rainy nights, mainly because spotlighting, as with a lot of other types of birding, is about using your ears. Even if a night bird does call on a wet or windy night, it's unlikely you will hear it, and there is no chance you will ever get onto it by listening for its movements in the foliage.

While you do get some owl freaks who spend all night roaming the bush by themselves, the chances are, when you go spotlighting, it will be with others, an advantage for safety reasons, and because the maxim 'Two sets of eyes are better than one' holds even more true in the dark.

There are, however, some pitfalls in spotlighting with a group. The following are the types of spotlighting companions it is best to avoid.

The incessant chatterer

Whether it be the excitement of the occasion (and no one is harder to shut up than an over-excited bird-nerd), or because there is some primeval throwback that spooks some people at night, causing them to become chatty when enveloped in darkness – as if, in the absence of a visual cue, they need to make a noise to confirm their own existence – these people are very likely to make any night creature scurry away well before they are in range of your spotlight beam.

The premature illuminator

Just as birds can hear you coming from a mile off, they can also see you, especially if you have somebody in your party that can't help but turn the spot on every five seconds. This is the premature illuminator. Too gung-ho for their own good, the premature illuminator constantly turns the spot on to what turns out to be leaves, rocks, insects, or the other members of the party turning around to yell, 'Stop turning that friggin' light on!'

The freaked-out urban dweller

Some people are so scared of snakes, spiders and tree roots or loose stones that might cause them to twist their ankle that they constantly turn on the light to check the terrain. It's a vicious cycle, for the more they have the light on, the less their eyes adjust to the dark, and the more they *need* a light on. One solution is to get them to hold the beam down towards the ground immediately in front so that there is not too much light spillage, or even better, take a small pen torch with them for the purpose.

The fat sniffler

These people are not necessarily fat, just their sniffles, which in the dark seem to be magnified tenfold. They probably won't drive away any potential spotlight targets, but will drive everybody else mad.

The poor aim

There is an art to spotlighting, and it is not simply a case of spraying the beam about like a shaky uncle at a toilet bowl after Christmas drinks, hoping to connect with something. The key is to look for eyeshine. All but a few creatures have a distinctive eyeshine (the Owlet-nightjar being a notable exception – it has eyes like black holes that seem to absorb light). To best pick up eyeshine, it helps to have the beam directly in front of your eyeline. Shooting a beam from the hip may look cool, but the anoraked Clint Eastwood will be missing out on a hell of a lot of eyeshine.

The gear freak

A gear freak will be so caught up with his night-vision goggles and whiz-bang paraphernalia that he'll usually miss the bird. A gear freak cost me my first White-throated Nightjar. It took so long to assemble his kit that I thought we'd missed our opportunity. When the silhouette of a nightjar did finally emerge out of the gloom, the gear freak flicked his switch. Nothing happened. He had forgotten to connect the spotlight to the battery (*see* GEAR FREAK).

 ACTION: In order to avoid retina burn, tape a sheet of red or blue plastic gel over your spotlight. These colours are thought to be less disturbing to the birds than a naked white light.

Spring / officially the season in Australia from 1 September to 30 November, but by that first day in September many of the spring migrants have been here for weeks, and in the south-west and the south-east many species have already mated and are beginning to build nests, or may even have young.

Spring is when the migratory waders begin to trickle in. Some gather at staging grounds such as the mudflats near Broome before they begin to head south. Others seem to come fairly directly. The Latham's Snipe are said to arrive in Victoria at the August full moon which suggests they don't dawdle, as they only start to leave their breeding grounds in Japan from the end of July onwards.

The waters remain cold and spring is often an even better time for southern pelagics than winter, though trips are cancelled more often at this time of year due to capricous winds. The breeding seabirds start to return. At first it's just a few, but later in September and October they come (in the case of the Short-tailed Shearwater, at least) in their millions. In some years conditions push the returning New Zealand breeders such as Mottled Petrel closer to our shores and for a few days we get a feast of these rarely encountered species.

In the north, conditions are at their toughest. It hasn't rained since last wet season and the parched land is crying out for a drink. The temperatures rise over the weeks, the humidity builds, massive thunderstorms play out a spectacular end to the day, but still no rain comes. You'd have to be mad to be out in a climate like this, yet as the tourist traps wind down for the season, a few birders venture forth in the hope of something unusual turning up in the form of overshooting Asian visitors such as wagtails, flycatchers and other rarities.

And while the nation is preoccupied with football finals, and then the spring racing carnival, the birding community rejoices that some old friends, the Koels and Rainbow Bee-eaters and Satin Flycatchers have made it back for another year. It's said that the Rufous Fantail always returns to the forests of Victoria on Melbourne Cup weekend, but I suspect that was the first weekend that the old birder who originated the myth actually went out to look for them.

Stalking / what birders are often charged with as they creep around in their anoraks and binoculars. 'Honestly, officer, I wasn't looking through that woman's window, I was looking at the hole in the wall above her window where I suspect a pardalote might be nesting!'

There are some basic pointers to bear in mind when stalking a bird of the feathered kind (*see* UNCLE TREVOR) so as to get a close or tickable view :

1. Move slowly and without sudden movements. The worst possible sudden movement is to point at the bird because to a bird, when a human is pointing something at it, it is usually shot or speared soon after.

2. If you have to talk, do so in a soft voice or whisper. Many birds don't seem to be too spooked by the human voice so long as it isn't sudden bursts of noise. I was in New Zealand hoping to see the New Zealand Storm-Petrel not long after it was rediscovered (it was thought extinct for 170 years). As the bird approached the boat, such an enormous cheer of exultation went up that the bird promptly turned around and flew away from us.

3. Wear clothing of muted colours. You may not need to go to full jungle greens (*see* CAMOUFLAGE), but when stalking a bird you are trying to attract the least amount of attention to yourself. This is why circus clowns make very poor birders; they dress loudly in every sense of the word, both in their choice of colours and the fact that their dicky lapels flap up into their face, their bow ties spin and their red noses honk loudly.

4. Try to keep down low. A bird is likely to be spooked by your silhouette breaking the horizon.

5. If you are using a telescope, hold the tripod out in front of you to break up your silhouette.

6. Approach slowly and perhaps not even directly. This will help the bird to get used to you. Amble around, pretend you're not interested, then casually sidle up to the bird and feign a yawn. It never worked for me as a teenager but perhaps birds aren't as cluey as my dates were.

7. Once you've got close enough for a satisfactory view or photograph, don't undo all your good work by simply standing up and walking off. It is discourteous, both to the bird and to other birdwatchers who are to follow. Once the bird has been spooked it will be much harder for the next person to get close to it.

8. And while we are on the subject of courtesy, respect other people's stalking. I was at Lake Connewarre near Geelong with a couple of birders twitching a Baird's Sandpiper (the fourth officially accepted Australian record). We had all had decent, tickable mid-range views. One of the party decided to try and photograph it. He spent the next 20 minutes painstakingly crawling on his belly through stinking mud trying to get close enough for a good photo. Our other companion went back to the car, got out his camera and simply walked up

behind the first photographer. The Baird's Sandpiper flushed (*see* FLUSH), leaving one extremely pissed off (and very muddy) twitcher.

 ACTION: Some birders have neither the patience nor the empathy to be able to stalk a bird. Try not to go birding with such people when going after a particularly flighty bird as even long instructions on how vital it is to keep still will only have an effect of 2.73 minutes, according to Big Twitch Institute research.

Stint Wars / a 1970s battle between two birding factions over the identity of some stints (a species of small migratory wading bird), which actually came to blows out at Werribee Sewage Farm.

Well 'blows' may be an exaggeration but there was rough physical contact – thereby making it the first official nerd war in history, preceding the Apple–Microsoft conflict by several years. Imagine two gangs of anorak-clad warriors hurling abuse at each other, tripods at the ready …

As immensely comic as they now seem, the Stint Wars, along with the Cox's Sandpiper affair (*see* COX'S SANDPIPER) mark a maturation of the Australian birding scene; one where it emerges from a fierce parochialism to a more open international approach to birds and birding, recognising that though isolated, we are still part of a global system.

POSTSCRIPT: Of the birds that the Stint Wars were fought over, one, the Little Stint, is now recognised as a regular, though extremely rare, visitor to our shores, while the other, the Temminck's Stint, has never been confirmed in this country since.

Stringer / **1.** a birder who attempts to claim a bird that they haven't actually seen, most often by trying to turn a comparatively common bird into something far rarer. **2.** anybody who has seen a bird that I have dipped on (*see* DIP).

To be labelled a stringer is about the worst accusation that can be thrown at a birder, as a reputation for honesty is paramount in a hobby where very often there is no way to prove what you have seen (*see* VERIFICATION).

A stringer 'strings' a bird. The first thing to clarify is that merely misidentifying a bird is not necessarily the same as stringing it. There is nothing particularly wrong with misidentifying a bird – even the best birders sometimes get it wrong. I actually find that the best birders will own up to their mistakes, no matter how embarrassing they may have been at the time. Where misidentification merges into stringing is when the birder maintains the fiction of the alleged sighting.

This implies that stringing is a deliberate act, but I always found it hard to believe that birders would be deliberately fraudulent when it came to claiming sightings of birds. I always assumed that the first person to be sucked in by string was the stringer themselves; that they had first convinced themselves of what they had seen.

This is actually pretty easy to do. With a lot of birds, views are not optimal. A half-glimpsed bird flying off from the side of the road as a carload of four birders speeds past can quite easily elicit four different calls as to what the species was. Everyone gets a slightly different perspective on the bird and, from the fragments of a glimpse, constructs the rest of the pieces together in their head. It doesn't take much to forget which was the bit of the bird that was actually seen and which was the part that was imagined. Usually in group circumstances such as this the identity of the bird is nutted out between the birders as they all add their impressions until consensus is reached. In circumstances such as this the truth usually will out. Stringing is an art best performed solo; the individual threads of a group string tend to tangle so that group stringing is rare.

Where group string (perhaps 'rope' would be the appropriate phrase?) does occur is where there is a combination of a dominant personality and more experienced birder who can impose his will upon a more compliant group. Or it can happen where the individual members of the group all want a bird to be something so badly that they all cajole each other into going that little bit further into stringing territory.

I recently almost fell into this trap. I have never seen a Grey Falcon (*see* GREY FALCON) so when word came from a reliable source of a probable Grey Falcon down at Werribee Sewage Farm (*see* WERRIBEE SEWAGE FARM) I contrived to take a morning off (much to my editor's chagrin) to look for this mythical beast.

Naturally I failed to get a sniff of it, and after a couple of hours spent scanning every likely perch I could find, I began to head home. As I drove out of the Farm, I passed three carloads of birders gathered by the side of the road. I backed up and greeted them with the traditional birders' salutation, 'Anything about?' They nodded vigorously and said, 'Grey Falcon!' I was out of the car like a shot, eager for more gen on this extraordinary turn of developments.

Only one of the birders had seen the bird and he had managed to photograph it before it flew off, only ten minutes earlier. He was still visibly shaking as he showed me the digital image on the back of his camera. The bird he showed me was a falcon and indeed it was grey, very grey. The others were all so excited, that I had no doubt that this was a Grey Falcon. I *wanted* to believe it was a Grey Falcon.

We all set off to scan even harder for where the bird could be roosting. All the time there was something nagging at me. The bird in the photo had a rather dark crown, which didn't sit right for Grey Falcon.

I caught up with the others and, expressing some doubts, asked to see the photo again. The dark crown was explained away to me as a trick of the light and when you saw the photo in decent light, it blended with the rest of the pale grey upperparts. I left them, still with some doubts, asking if the photographer could email me a copy later.

The bird in question was never seen again.

Later that night when I received the emailed photo, it was instantly clear on the computer screen that it was in fact not a Grey Falcon but a rather pale-backed Peregrine Falcon. I am not for a moment saying that the original photographer was trying to string a Grey Falcon. He had merely misidentified a Peregrine. I had so wanted it to be a Grey Falcon, and was so swayed by the enthusiasm of the group, that I was the one who almost stringed it because I came very close to perpetuating a misidentification.

For years I thought that this was how stringing originated: in the observer's enthusiasm for putting together pieces of a bird that were never actually there. I think there are certain types of people, or more accurately, certain approaches to birding that lend themselves to stringing. For instance, there are two very similar types of owls, the Barn Owl and the Masked Owl. If a non-string prone birder flushed one from the side of the road and only had a split second glimpse, he might not be sure of the ID, but on the view he had, would say there was a 90 per cent chance of it being the far more common Barn Owl. On the same view, the susceptible-to-string character would think that there was a ten per cent chance it was the rarer Masked Owl.

From one perspective the bird would go down in the notebook as a 'probable Barn Owl'; in the other a 'possible Masked Owl'. It is then a much shorter step to string that owl into a Masked, because birder number two is now seemingly legitimately saying to himself, 'well it could have been a Masked Owl, so why wasn't it?', whereas that leap is too wide for the first birder who is now thinking more along the lines of, 'That owl looked a bit funny, but I doubt it could have been anything other than a Barn'.

But the longer I have been around birders, the more I am coming to suspect that the odd one will occasionally string a bird deliberately. I have the feeling that certain types of personalities hate to be wrong and, rather than lose face over a bad call, will persist in defending a mistake with a passion.

One does not throw the term 'stringer' around lightly in the bird world, as it is a devastating label to be saddled with, but even if you were absolutely convinced that somebody was stringing something, if you were to call them on it it would be the one time they were actually telling the truth and really did have a Fiordland Crested Penguin swim a couple of hundred kilometres up a river and appear in front of them at an inland irrigation channel. I hope this far-fetched example has never actually happened as the person who did find such a penguin would think I was labelling them a stringer!

Summer / in Australia, officially from 1 December to 28 February; also known as birdwatching season. Actually, most times of the year are birdwatching seasons; it's just that birders, like the rest of the population, tend to have more holidays over summer, hence they have more time to go birding.

In reality, summer conditions have usually been in force over most of Australia from early November and they often last through well into March. Across the north, the summer wet season often doesn't really kick in until the end of year or the beginning of the next. Sometimes it doesn't really happen at all.

When the wet hits with full force, there is a glorious profusion of life. Many birds start to breed with a vengeance, and the waterbirds that had been concentrated at the few remaining waterholes spread across the ever-expanding floodplains.

From the north to the south, summer is the time of vagrants. The overshooters from Indonesia and the genuine strays from further afield in Asia or even the Americas turn up unexpectedly far more often in summer than at any other time of the year.

Along the east, south and south-west coasts, many birds have finished breeding. The forests and woodlands are quieter now that the males aren't advertising for mates and defending their territories so vigorously.

The inland swamps dry up, sending a mass exodus of waterfowl, waterbirds and waders to the coastal regions where, with a bit of luck, the water lasts a lot longer. This is the time of year when birders in the big cities don't have to go too far to get some excellent birding done.

Summer certainly is a great time of year for the birder. And if we're really lucky a couple of big cyclones brew up out of the Indian Ocean and throw down not just a mass of rain when they hit the land mass, but also bucketloads of Asian vagrants (*see* VAGRANT). Some years they have hit the deck as far south as Kalgoorlie. Only a twitcher would book a holiday to Broome after seeing the weather chart showing a big low brewing up cyclonic conditions, but if you want to find a rare Asian swiftlet, that's the time to do it!

Suppressor / a birder who fails to tell others about a rare bird they have sighted; next to being a stringer, the suppressor is the lowest of the low in the twitching universe.

The whole point of twitching is to see new birds. So when twitchers find out somebody knew about a twitchable rarity and didn't tell them, there is no forgiveness, even if the suppression was done for the welfare of the bird, such as protecting its nesting site from being trampled. Twitching and paranoia are often bedfellows, so if it is a fellow twitcher who has withheld the information, then the conspiracy theories kick in and the twitcher will become convinced that they were kept out of the loop primarily to prevent them from catching up to the other twitcher's list. And sometimes, they may well be right . . .

Tasmania / the island state that has a reputation for being clean, green and friendly; also the state with the highest percentage of its old-growth forests being woodchipped, and the only place where I have ever been threatened with being shot for going birdwatching.

Our smallest state, Tasmania, not surprisingly, has the smallest bird list (aside from the ACT which is not technically a state), with around 320 species having been recorded.

At it has been isolated for so long, Tassie does have a good number of endemic species (twelve) with another two, the Swift and Orange-bellied Parrots, only breeding on the island and then migrating to the mainland. This represents an endemism rate higher than Queensland's, though Queensland does have double the number of birds found nowhere else in Australia (but not necessarily elsewhere in the world). Tasmania has some of the best seabirding in the country; the continental shelf is not far offshore so there is easy access to the deeper water species, and, due to its southerly location, the Apple Isle gets far more sub-Antarctic seabirds, such as the Grey Petrel and Southern Fulmar passing through. Pelagics out of the east coast from places like St Helens and Eaglehawk Neck can often go out in bad weather that elsewhere would lead to the trip being cancelled, yet here the land mass tends to shield the offshore waters from the prevailing south-westerly winds.

Though it is compact, much of Tasmania is rather inaccessible. Luckily for birders most of the hot spots are very close to the main population centres. Places well worth checking out include Bruny and Maria Islands, and areas around Hobart such as Fern Tree, Peter Murrell Reserve, Lauderdale and Barilla Bay, the last two throwing up an interesting wader every now and then. Also good for birds, including some of the more exotic plastics, are Flinders Island and (especially) King Island in Bass Strait.

The birding population on the island is small but enthusiastic, and like everything else in Tasmania travels along quite self-sufficiently without getting too much attention from the rest of the country. These birders welcome visitors warmly, but I get the impression that if you see something unusual in Tasmania your sighting will be regarded with even more than the usual skepticism, because you are an outsider and they are very protective of 'their' birds. Then again, they probably hear all sorts of rubbish claimed by visitors who haven't bothered to work out what bird is meant to be in Tassie and what doesn't make it there.

 ACTION: The prime birdwatching body in the state is Birds Tasmania, which can be contacted at:

> The Secretary
> Birds Tasmania
> GPO Box 68
> Hobart,
> Tasmania 7001

Taxonomy / the classification of birds into a specific order.

Often the taxonomy a birder follows determines the size of their list as much as the number of actual birds they have seen. There are several taxonomic lists of Australian birds, some compiled by international scientists, some locally. If you go by one taxonomy you may have a total of 732 species on your list, but using another may drop the total substantially, or increase it. It would certainly make a difference if you thought your total was 700 and another taxonomy dropped you out of the 700 Club.

The taxonomy Australian birders generally follow is that of Christidis and Boles, with a new version to come out very soon (*see* CHECKLISTS). I don't really know whether it is any better than others, such as the one produced for the CSIRO by Schodde and Mason, but I follow the consensus opinion as I prefer to compare like against like.

The one thing that is not kosher is to mix and match the different checklists to optimise your list. Once you choose to follow one, you are stuck with it, I'm afraid. For better or worse, in stringiness and in health.

Telescope / not as essential for birding as binoculars, but a 'scope' comes in very handy, particularly when looking for waders or waterbirds or when on a land-based sea watch (*see* SEA WATCH, WADER).

Telescopes are practically unusable for watching seabirds on a pelagic trip as you will never get conditions that allow you to hold your scope steady. The same goes for most bush birding, where the distances are usually so short you won't even be able to focus your scope.

For the same reasons, do not get fooled into purchasing too high-powered a telescope. Around 20–30 magnification is usually adequate. Anything greater and you will find you will have trouble focusing, and even the slightest breath of wind or movement will cause the image to shake dramatically. So astronomical telescopes are right out. Any scope designed to observe the rings of Saturn is not going to be much chop when trained on a godwit at a hundred paces.

It is amazing how much heat haze you pick up through a telescope. Even early in the morning when it doesn't feel hot, haze that you don't pick up with the naked eye can be so dense as to render the scope almost useless.

There are plenty of good brands out there with a range of prices. The best are those with polished lenses but these can cost an exorbitant amount. I use a spotting scope, which is a more compact design and can be stored in a suitcase more easily than some of the larger models.

For a while I didn't have a tripod for my scope, which meant that I would have to prop it up on fencepost, stump, or the top of my birding companion's head. Luckily I used to go birding with people with skulls as flat as an aircraft carrier, but I found they moved too often for satisfactory viewing.

There are more designs for tripod legs and clasps than there are for just about any bit of gear known to man. Some are more difficult to work out than a bookshelf from IKEA, and others have such vicious clasps holding the leg extensions in place that you are in mortal danger of losing a finger to them. The main problem with tripods is their weight. A simple piece of soft foam wrapped around the legs of your tripod is helpful in reducing the impact of its weight on your shoulders when you're carrying both your tripod and scope for long distances; I have recently taken to using a monopod, which is far easier to carry. It works surprisingly well, and though there is more shake than with a tripod, it is far more manoeuvrable. The big drawback with the monopod is that it is no good for showing other people something through your scope, whereas a tripod, with its fixed position, enables you to line a bird up and the next person gets the exactly the same view.

 ACTION: When walking with a scope it is a good idea not to have the legs of the tripod fully extended as they can become rather cumbersome, catching in the wind, on fences, or on fellow birders. But, as you don't want to be continually extending and folding up the legs, I find it is best to have the legs extended halfway, with the section closest to your body (the top extension) fully extended. This means you only have to extend one section when you put the scope down to use, and it can usually be done while the tripod is still on your shoulder.

Tertials / the innermost of the flight feathers on a bird, sometimes known as the tertiary feathers. The outermost flight feathers are called the primaries, and the ones between them and the tertials are, not surprisingly, called the secondaries.

The tertials are the flight feathers closest to the body (usually three – despite what some books say, there can be more than three, as with waders and gulls and terns). When a bird is at rest, most of the other flight feathers tuck up beneath the tertials, protected from the elements. In flight the tertials are barely noticeable, but when a bird is at rest, the tertials are often all that you see of the flight feathers.

If you want to come across seriously as a birdwatcher, then 'tertials' is a term you will not only have to become familiar with but should invoke at every opportunity. The correct (and frequent) use of the word will do more to add to your cachet as a genuine player than anything else you can ever do or say. Merely knowing the term and when to apply it says to the world that you know birds, oh yes, do you know birds.

In native Australian birds, the tertials are comparatively small and undeveloped compared with their Northern Hemisphere counterparts. This is probably because most families of Australian birds have evolved without the need for substantial migration. Birds that undertake long-distance migration are usually endowed with much longer and stronger wings. For these species the tertials have to be longer to cover the elongated flight feathers, a function even more important for birds that need to keep their flight feathers well protected in order to be able to make their remarkable journeys.

The lack of obvious tertials in birds such as honeyeaters, thornbills and fairy-wrens has made Australian birders almost completely ignorant of the importance of tertials. But in identifying our vagrant species, most of which are Northern Hemisphere birds that have overshot on migration, a knowledge of tertials is essential. The Red-throated Pipit, for example (two confirmed records), is almost indistinguishable from the Pechora Pipit (one record) in non-breeding plumage – except for the tertials: they are a dead giveaway. One of the key features that separates a Little Stint from the regular Red-necked Stint is the 'foxy' red fringes to the tertials.

The trouble is that even finding the tertials is difficult enough. I am a good enough birdwatcher to know that I should be looking for them, but I quickly realise that I am not quite the gun twitcher I imagine myself to be when, as often as not, I struggle even to locate where they are on a bird. I guess I must suffer from a medical condition known as tertial blind-spot syndrome.

ACTION: To make yourself look like the real deal, throw in a statement like, 'Mmm, there's something funny about the tertials on this plover' when you are birding with a group of wader experts. As long as you make sure you are looking at a plover when you say it, you are guaranteed to win instant respect from your companions because a) you know that tertials exist, b) you recognise that they are important and presumably you have been scrutinising the tertials on every bird you are looking at, and c) by saying they look 'funny' you are indicating that you know what normal tertials look like. The beauty of this is that 'funny' is such a vague and subjective term that, even if challenged, you can rebut with, 'Yeah, you're probably right, but I dunno; they seemed a bit funny.' And there is more than a 50/50 chance that the tertials will look funny, because they are likely to be missing or worn or growing back after moult. Your companions think you are the real deal, and you haven't risked exposing your ignorance.

Tick / what the beauteous and wondrous creature that is a bird is reduced to in a birder's check-list.

The essential goal of twitching is to get as many ticks on your list as possible (see CHECKLIST, LIST, RULES OF TWITCHING).

Ticker / another name for a twitcher (*see* TWITCHER), someone obsessed with ticking off new birds on their list.

Also known as a lister, arising from a birder's obsession with the size of their list; and also annoying prat, because, well, someone going on about nothing but the size of their list really can be an annoying prat.

Twitch / 1. the involuntary, jerky, physical movements of a birder when they hear of a bird turning up that they haven't seen. 2. the act of chasing after said bird so as to add it to a birder's list.

Though many think that the former is the origin of the word 'twitch', it actually comes from two English birders in the early days of the modern birding era. These two chaps, who by all accounts are rather embarrassed at having inspired the term, used to drive across the country chasing rare birds on a motorbike with a pillion seat. As this was England, they inevitably arrived at their destination shivering madly from the cold. Other birders joked that they always appeared to be twitching when they saw a new bird. Soon, the act of chasing a rare bird became known as 'going on a twitch', and the name stuck (*see* TWITCHER).

Twitchathon / 1. a 24-hour bird race run by various Birds Australia regional groups as a fundraiser. Teams seek sponsorship for every bird that they manage to see or hear as a team within a state or regional boundary in a designated 24-hour period. 2. an elite sport that deserves to be included as part of the Olympic Games.

For some sad twitchers (like me), this is the highlight of the birding calendar, and way too much time is spent in preparation and strategising for the event. There are two main theories on how to approach a Twitchathon:

1. To cover as many habitats as possible in order to maximise your chances of seeing a wide suite of species.

2. To cover fewer habitats more thoroughly, spending longer at each site so as to have a better chance of seeing all the species that are there.

Our Twitchathon team chooses an extreme version of the former – in covering as many habitats as possible we often drive up to 1200 kilometres, which essentially means that we spend more time in the car driving to the birds than we do actually looking at them! We only stop to refuel and try not to stop to eat, sleep or go to the toilet. It is a rather stupid thing to do when you look at it in the cold hard light of day, but I find it the most enjoyable sporting event I have ever participated in, because no matter how you clothe it in noble intentions (fundraising for the environment, putting into place the knowledge learned about birds and the habitats they need to survive) it is a down-and-dirty competition pure and simple.

Rather than trying to explain or justify the lure of a Twitchathon to you, I will simply give a brief summary of our team's November 2006 Twitchathon attempt and let you decide for yourself – exciting or stupid, sport or sheer madness. (Locations have been suppressed in order not to give too much away to our competitiors.)

SATURDAY

1600: UNDISCLOSED COASTAL LOCATION

We start at a popular seaside resort a couple of hours' drive south of Melbourne. Arriving at a lookout with 20 minutes before the start, the team locates some key species and sets up telescopes on each of them so that we waste no time getting started. Once this is done we scan the ocean for any passing seabirds and pray that they hang around long enough to be counted once the race gets under way. One year we had a Shy Albatross disappear over the horizon just seconds before the four o'clock starting time.

This year we line up Kelp Gull, Sooty Oystercatcher and Black-faced Cormorant in the scopes, but there is no sign of the Peregrine Falcons that breed on the cliff-face opposite. We are one bird down before the race has even begun. Luckily, there are a couple of obvious Little Penguins sitting at the end of their burrows. We don't want to repeat the year in which we could only find one and couldn't tell if it was alive or dead. One of us had to poke it to make sure it was still kicking.

The time on the GPS device ticks over to four. Like a production line we each take a view at each bird through a scope until the majority of the team have ticked it so that it officially counts. Sooty Oik? Tick! Kelp Gull? Tick! Black-faced Cormorant? Tick! And we're off!

After an hour and a half at the coastal location (including a dash up a heavily populated surf beach laden with telescopes looking for the Hooded Plovers who weren't in their usual spot) we are off with 70 species under the belt, four more than our previous best.

1844: ARRIVE AT UNDISCLOSED FOREST LOCATION

After adding thirteen more species along the way, we hit the wet forests and manage to lock onto some great, hard-to-get species such as Southern Emu-wren, Blue-winged Parrot, Superb Lyrebird and Brush Cuckoo. We bird until dark and then start hunting for owls. This forest is usually crawling with them, but as the rules forbid the use of tapes to call them in, it's a matter of waiting and listening. We hear Sooty and Boobook Owls but that's about it. Only two of us hear the only White-throated Nightjar of the night, as the other two are fossicking about in the car for some tucker. Next year we may ban food altogether!

By the time we leave the forest at 2205 we have 114 species, still five ahead of our best-ever total.

2227: SMALL WETLAND IN NEW SUBURBAN HOUSING DEVELOPMENT

We've stopped at this location for the first time but we fail to get any of our target species. I look at the map and realise we are at the wrong small suburban wetland. With no time to check the other one out, we head on into Melbourne.

2322: CENTRAL MELBOURNE LOCATION

Within kicking distance of the CBD we add Tawny Frogmouth and Nankeen Night Heron at our ever-reliable sites. The only trouble is that to get here takes a long detour off the freeway. If we found a site out in the country for these two species we could easily save ourselves a good 20 minutes.

SUNDAY 0300: UNDISCLOSED NORTHERN VICTORIAN GRASSLAND

In a cruel irony, the first rain in over a month decides to fall this night, making access to some sites impossible and keeping many of the nightbirds we were expecting quiet. Our trudge around the native grasslands in the drizzle is rewarded when we hear the booming call of the exceptionally rare Plains-wanderer.

0402: UNDISCLOSED NORTHERN VICTORIAN WETLAND

The rain has made the track into this wetland impassable, so we slip and slide our way down the entrance road on foot, the mud piling on the soles of our boots until they are like high-heeled clogs. We dip on the guaranteed Little Bittern, but do manage to hear the boom of the Australasian Bittern, a sound so haunting it fuelled the bunyip myth.

0550: ARRIVE AT CLASSIFIED HIGHWAY LOCATION (APPROXIMATELY 350 KM NORTH OF MELBOURNE)

We are 20 minutes behind schedule but with so much rain and black cloud around, it's not light enough in the pre-dawn to do any birding anyway. We come to this spot specifically because it is the most southerly colony of Chestnut-crowned Babblers we can find, but once it is light enough to bird, they are nowhere to be found.

0639: ARRIVE AT MALLEE SITE

It is raining so hard that we are forced to abandon a couple of quick stops, which puts us back on schedule but down a couple of species. Our prime site proves to be outstanding, with all the regulars such as Splendid Fairy-wren and Mulga Parrot plus new birds for our Twitchathon route, White-fronted and Striped Honeyeaters. We depart, still on track for our best-ever total, at 0719.

0801: ARRIVE AT ANOTHER UNDISCLOSED WETLAND SITE, NORTHERN VICTORIA

After wasting five precious minutes trying unsuccessfully to track down Zebra Finch which we later see anyway, we arrive at our planned wetland site. It is here the wheels begin to fall off. The worst drought on record has seen most wetland birds abandon the area, so that even the few wetlands with any water in them are bereft of some key species – they have all gone down to Werribee, where coincidentally on this particular day all the other teams are birding in perfect conditions. We are still battling rain and finding that many birds have deserted us. The list only kicks along by seven at this site to take us up to 161, birds we could have easily seen at Werribee, like the Greenshank, Wood and Curlew Sandpiper and Black-tailed Godwit, fall by the wayside.

1110: ARRIVE AT MYSTERY MURRAY RIVER LOCATION
By the time we hit the red gum forests we are about five behind our best total for the equivalent stage, but have added a couple of handy birds to the total, including White-bellied Sea-Eagle, Latham's Snipe and Grey-crowned Babbler.

The red gum forests prove to be a disaster. We see next to none of our expected birds and waste too much time not seeing them. We compensate somewhat at our next location, Terrick Terrick National Park, which has never let us down, and we leave there on 198 species. Our best-ever result was 211 and we now have 3 1/4 hours to beat it.

1322: ARRIVE AT SECRET MALLEE SITE
This is our last shot at some dry country birds, and it's excruciating. Ten years of drought have taken their toll. There hasn't been a successful breeding season in all those ten years and what was once a vibrant habitat is spookily quiet. While we miss out on only two or three hoped-for species, it takes us twice as long as normal to find the ones we are after, like Shy Heathwren (living up to its name), Tawny-crowned and Purple-gaped Honeyeaters and Inland Thornbill.

1542: ARRIVE AT UNDISCLOSED BOX-IRONBARK LOCATION
After grinding our way tediously through the Bendigo area, we arrive at our final birding site, in a Box-Ironbark forest with eighteen minutes to go and our total at 210, one behind our best-ever score.

We have a Square-tailed Kite's nest lined up, and after a small drama when we take the wrong track we are rewarded with one of the adults sitting on the nest at 1545. We have equalled our record.

Nothing else is about, so we head to a dam where we have had Spotless Crake calling before. As we wait by the dam, we tally the list and realise I have written down Eastern Yellow Robin twice. We are actually only at 210 species, with three minutes to go. Just then a Black-chinned Honeyeater calls, putting us back on 211.

The last two and a bit minutes are torture. We strain our ears but the forest is silent. We walk over to the edge of the forest, one of us remembering seeing a Speckled Warbler in similar habitat at a different location but what have we got to lose? Of course there are no warblers there.

The GPS begins its ten-second countdown to the finishing time. One of the guys sees a bird of prey through the trees and screams, 'Collared Sparrowhawk!' We scramble to see it. I get onto it seven beeps left and then, in a James Bond countdown clock finish, a third member sees the sparrowhawk with four beeps to go. (You only need a majority of the team to see or hear a bird for it to count.) We all high-five each other, delirious from the lack of sleep as the last shot of adrenaline drains from our bodies.

Another check of the list and we realise I hadn't added the Plains-wanderer from the night before. We ended up with 213 species after all, two clear of our previous best and three ahead of the second placegetters.

Oh, and after all that, our team raised over $500 for conservation projects.

 ACTION: Contact your local branch of Birds Australia (*see* BIRDS AUSTRALIA) for details of your state's twitchathon.

Twitcher / hard-core birders who, having run out of common species to add to their lists, go chasing after rare or vagrant species where and whenever they happen to turn up (*see* TWITCH).

Although the twitching scene in Australia is nowhere near as big as in England and many other countries, the media and public are becoming more familiar with the term and increasingly refer to all birdwatchers as twitchers. Many birders don't appreciate the label, viewing twitching with a kind of moral repugnance. Nothing more than birding stamp-collectors, only concerned with selfishly growing their lists, twitchers do little actually to help birds or to add to the body of scientific knowledge. Their obsession gives all other birders a bad name. These are all accusations commonly levelled at twitchers from within the birding community itself. And as a self-professed twitcher I am often forced to defend twitching and twitchers, but I have to say, I can see where the detractors are coming from. Consider how it must feel for the ordinary birdwatcher. They go out birding regularly and while they clearly get a lot of enjoyment out of it, they put in the hard yards, doing local surveys, getting out there on a regular basis and working hard for the birds. Then one day, they see a rare bird on their local patch, say perhaps a Purple Heron (which would be a first for Australia). Suddenly the local birder is inundated with calls. Within 24 hours of word getting out, the first twitchers descend on the town. Edgy and anxious until they have seen the bird, they disappear once they have it ticked off, often without a word of thanks.

Still the calls keep coming. Was the bird there this morning? Where's the nearest airport? Where can I stay? The local birder has people sleeping on the floor. Neighbours are reporting strange men sleeping in cars parked out the front of their house. One old lady has the life frightened out of her by a man emerging from the bushes at dawn dressed in camouflage gear, with a camera that has a lens the size of a bazooka. The lovely little wetland patch ends up being trampled by desperate twitchers when the heron fails to show one morning.

It is easy to see these twitchers as birdwatching vultures, just circling around waiting to feed on somebody else's bird. Fortunately, the behaviour I've described is actually quite rare in Australia and only a very few twitchers can legitimately be characterised as being only interested in adding ticks to their lists.

Many twitchers actually work in the conservation field or spend countless unpaid hours studying birds and contributing to the general field of knowledge about them.

In a country that vastly underfunds conservation management, it is the work of amateurs that gives us the bulk of the raw data about our birds. It is often the much-maligned twitchers doing the surveys and researching identification and distribution who provide so much crucial information for our conservation managers.

What people tend to forget is that birdwatching is a hobby, entered into by its participants for their own enjoyment. To me, twitching is the game I like to play. Some turn up their noses at it, saying if they want to see a Purple Heron they would much prefer to go to Asia and see hundreds of them in their natural habitat, not some anomaly with a poor sense of direction. And to them I say, if that is the game you prefer, then that is fine. I am an Aussie Rules fan and soccer does little for me, but that doesn't mean I begrudge the people who enjoy watching the world game. I have no problem with both of them existing. But to such a person I would point out that if you were a Deep Purple fan (continuing the purple theme) and they came out to Australia to play, would you not go see them because they were not in their native England? Surely, seeing them play on your home turf makes the occasion even more exciting. For me, seeing a bird that shouldn't be here is part of the appeal, and while I have seen Purple Herons in both Singapore and Spain where they are meant to be, I reckon I would still get more excitement seeing one in a swamp in outback Queensland after having driven two days to get there, all the time not knowing whether it would still be there when I arrived. That to me, is about as exciting as birding can get.

But then, I am just a little bit strange.

Two-bird theory / where there is a disagreement over the identification of a bird, it may be explained by the theory that each observer actually saw a different bird to the other, and therefore both of them were correct.

The two-bird theory is often the only way to settle a dispute and leave both parties with their dignity intact. Sometimes it does actually happen, particularly on a sea watch where there is an awful lot of sea in which to try and find the same bird (*see* SEA WATCHING), but most of the time, people are just being diplomatic when they invoke the theory.

Uncle Trevor / the laugh-at-their-own-jokes type of bloke who lives for the chance to lob in a ribald double entendre at every opportunity; everybody has an Uncle Trevor in their life, be it an actual uncle, a distant relative, or a workmate.

For a birdwatcher, life is full of Uncle Trevors. If I had a dollar coin for every time an Uncle Trev type has told me with a wink and a nod, 'Birdwatching, hey? I'm a bit of a BIRDWATCHER myself, if you know what I mean!', I'd pelt every single one of those coins at Uncle Trevor's grinning mug.

 ACTION: For all the aspiring Uncle Trevors reading this book I put out this challenge: how many double entendres can you spot in this book? A quick glance by me identified 24 clear instances where the word 'bird' appears in a potentially saucy context, not to mention all the times I refer to things like boobies, tits and shags. See? The hilarity never ceases.

Upland Sandpiper / a peculiar long-necked, small-headed North American wader that has only ever been recorded once in Australia.

Any birder who saw the original Upland Sandpiper would be very pleased with themselves. Not only has it never turned up again, they would be at least 170 years old as the bird was shot near Sydney in 1848!

Urban birding / birdwatching in the cities and suburbs – it can be done.

The great thing about birds is that if there is a habitat niche they will fill it, and thus, even in the middle of our largest cities good numbers of birds can be found. And I am not just talking about the masses of feral pigeons that scurry about under your feet in the Bourke Streets or Rundle Malls. There are good native birds to be had right under the noses of millions of city commuters, an entire subculture operating under its own rules as we go about our business oblivious to it all.

Every major city or town has a botanic gardens and though they are often very European in design (Canberra's superb native gardens a notable exception) they can still attract a wide range of native species. I have seen Rufous Owls in Darwin's gardens, Powerful Owls in Melbourne's (they also turn up in Sydney's as well) and Great Bowerbirds in Townsville's. Other large parks can also be good, especially when they contain remnant native vegetation, King's Park in Perth being a prime example.

Most of our cities are situated on waterfronts of one kind or another and these areas, along with many ornamental ponds, can be good for waterbirds, particularly in drier years when they act as a drought refuge. Most birders who have seen the elusive Little Bittern have done so not at the inland swamps they typically call home, but in tiny reed-fringed ponds in the middle of suburbia, such as Sherwood Park in Brisbane (which is also a reliable site for Bush-hen) and Centennial Park in Sydney.

Some of the country's best wader watching sites are on the doorstep of our cities, none more so than the Esplanade in Cairns. Most tourists are disappointed when they arrive at the Cairns foreshore, as it is all mudflats and not a grain of sparkling golden sand. The birder revels in it and is able to get up-close views of a huge variety of waders, with the only risk being a collision with a speeding rollerblader.

It is even possible to get some great seabirding in without having to leave metropolitan Sydney where from the cliffs of the eastern suburbs it is not unusual to spy Wandering and other Albatross, huge rafts of Wedge-tailed Shearwaters and many other goodies. Both Sydney and Melbourne have Little Penguin colonies within a few kilometres of the CBD, although not only do the penguins have to compete with extra pollution, predators and speeding motor craft, they also have to endure attacks from utter morons who are in serious need of mental help, or a good shock with a cattle prod.

Surprisingly our suburbs can be useful for threatened species as well. Swift Parrots utilise flowering eucalypts in Hobart and Melbourne gardens as well as those of many smaller towns from Maryborough in Victoria to Toowoomba in Queensland. And in 2002 the only recorded breeding event in the entire country for the elusive Painted Snipe was in a small swamp created by a leaky pipe in the middle of a Gold Coast development.

There are, however, a few drawbacks with urban birding that you don't usually get birding anywhere else. Foremost is that the places that attract birds – quiet, leafy, out of the way places – also attract other forms of life that like to operate out of sight. You won't often stumble on a drug deal or anything too criminal, but it is something to be wary of.

What is more likely is that your urban birding meanderings will take you into the heart of a gay beat. It has happened to me at Melbourne's ironically named Studley Park one lunchtime, where the office workers and tradesmen gathered for a bit of action took a sudden and unwanted interest in the kinky guy with binoculars around his neck; and also at a park alongside Canberra's Lake Burley Griffin where, right on dusk as we were looking for a Regent Honeyeater roost, a veritable Mardi Gras float full of repressed public servants emerged from the undergrowth looking for a roost of their own. Even in Alice Springs, where I was on my first major solo birding trip at the tender age of eighteen I was approached in a park. I was sitting, looking up into a Red Gum trying to turn a Striated Pardalote into a Red-browed, when a guy probably not much older than me approached and tried to turn me towards the public toilet block. He wouldn't take no for answer, and though probably harmless, he managed to totally freak me out as he followed me throughout the Alice Springs township for the rest of the day. (The town is not that big, especially if you are trying to shake someone trailing you.)

More likely to affect your urban birding session are the odd looks you'll get from other park users. Don't be surprised if you are called over by the police to explain why you are lurking about the park armed with high-powered optical equipment. At times like these I find it is best to play up your Asbirders tendencies and make out to be more of an idiot-savant than you really are. It raises less suspicion if people think you are simple.

For those who have only an hour or two to spare in one of our capital cities, here are a few places where you can make the most of your time.

Adelaide

Inner: Cleland Conservation Park – One of Adelaide's best-known parks, Cleland probably has the widest species range of the series of parks in the Mount Lofty Ranges.

Further out: Penrice Saltfields – Permission is needed to gain access, but this area is one of the country's greatest birding sites, with a remarkable number of vagrant waders turning up (*see* SEA VAGRANT).

Brisbane

Inner: Manly – While not as good as it was 20 or 30 years ago thanks to overdevelopment, the shores of Moreton Bay still hold a few good waders as well as some mangrove birds. At the suburb of Manly, an artificial wader roost has been constructed which, unlike many similar projects, seems actually to attract waders.

Further out: Mount Nebo – There are several small national parks in the Mount Nebo–Mount Glorious area containing some very nice patches of rainforest and their corresponding birds such as Noisy Pitta, Wompoo Fruit-Dove and Green Catbird.

Canberra

Inner: Jerrabomberra Wetlands – Situated next to the main sewage farm, these wetlands have some viewing areas for a sometimes surprisingly diverse range of species.

Further out: Tidbinbilla Nature Reserve – Though devastated by the 2003 bushfires, the area and its birds are making a comeback, and it should return to being one of the best places in the country to see the Superb Lyrebird.

Darwin

Inner: Buffalo Creek – The creek itself is a great site for mangrove species, including the elusive Chestnut Rail, while the nearby beach is a renowned wader site.

Further out: Howard Springs – A great croc-free swimming site, there is a patch of monsoon forest adjacent to the springs which is a brilliant spot for Rainbow Pitta and other Top End highlights like Rose-crowned Fruit-Dove.

Hobart

Inner: Fern Tree – A good site for the tricky to see Scrubtit. The nearby Waterworks Reserve is also good birding, as well as being great for mammals at night, with Masked Owl a possibility.

Further out: Peter Murrell Reserve is well known as a good spot for the rare endemic Forty-spotted Pardalote, but it is also contains other groovy birds such as Dusky Robin.

Melbourne

Inner: Williamstown – The mouth of Kororoit Creek near Williamstown is now part of the Jawbone Flora and Fauna Reserve, and while it doesn't have quite the amount of birdlife as wetlands a bit further afield like Werribee Sewage Farm and Point Cook, it is surprising what does turn up there.

Further out: The Edithvale–Seaford Wetlands are my local patch, the area where I cut my egg-teeth birdwatching. Both have a huge birdlist, including some real cripplers, but Edithvale has more facilities (*see* CRIPPLER). Not far away is Braeside Park which also has wetlands as well as some woodland and heathy areas.

Perth

Inner: Herdsman Lake – A wetland to the north of the city, well set up for visitors, many species of waterbirds can be seen very well.

Further out: Wungong Dam – Just beyond Perth's eastern suburban sprawl, Wungong is a great place for many of the south-west's endemics, including the highly sought-after Red-eared Firetail.

Sydney

Inner: Magic Point, Maroubra is a superb sea watching site, and the surrounding coastal heathland has in the past harboured some very nice birds, such as the Southern Emu-wren and Lewin's Rail, and in 2003, amazingly, an Orange-bellied Parrot turned up there (*see* SEA WATCHING).

Further out: Windsor – This region north-west of Sydney can be very good for wetland species, particularly some of the rarer waders, and the surrounding countryside contains many habitats from grassland to patches of wet forest.

Vagrant / a bird that turns up in a region where it shouldn't normally be.

Unlike its human counterpart, a vagrant bird is a stray that is always welcome, at least to a birdwatcher. Vagrants are also known as 'accidentals', and are often wrongly referred to as 'rarities'. Both a Dunlin and a Nordmann's Greenshank are considered vagrants when they are seen in Australia (both have only one accepted sighting each). In an Australian context they would be considered extreme rarities, but worldwide, the Dunlin is found in the hundreds of thousands if not millions, while the Nordmann's is down to a couple of thousand at best – a rarity in any sense of the word.

The appearance of a vagrant on our shores is what really gets a twitcher twitching, for it is these birds that will be new to a twitcher's list once all the local species have been seen. As soon as a vagrant is reported, twitchers across the country scramble to work out whether they can make the trip to see it (*see* TWITCH). Some places such as Broome or Ashmore Reef seem to be vagrant traps due, no doubt, to their proximity to migration destinations. But often a vagrant will turn up in the most unlikely of places, such as the dry cow paddock at Mount Carbine favoured by the Isabelline Wheatear, or the shopping centre in suburban Newcastle that Australia's fourth confirmed Black-backed Wagtail called home.

Verification / being able to prove that you did see a bird that you have claimed to have seen.

The question I am most often asked by non-birdwatchers when they find out I am into birding – apart from whether birds have penises (*see* GONADS) – is how I can prove that I have seen a bird. Or, to put it more bluntly, 'What's to say you just don't make it all up?'

The simple answer is that if nobody else was with me when I saw the bird and I wasn't able to take a photograph, film or sound recording, ultimately I can never definitively prove that I saw it.

This is where reputation becomes so crucial. Birding is often compared to golf in that a golfer can write down any score when out on the course alone, but once others notice that the supposed hot shot's scores aren't nearly as impressive when played in the company of others, that golfer will earn a dubious reputation and never be taken seriously again.

Personally, I can't see the point in claiming a bird when you know in all honesty that you probably haven't seen it – ultimately the main person you are cheating is yourself – but I know the temptation. Especially when you are starting out you really want to see a particular bird, so you push at the edges of what your conscience can take and birds sneak onto your list that you know really shouldn't be there – I was sure I had an Owlet-nightjar sitting on a power line when I was a kid, but the car was travelling at 100 kilometres an hour and Dad wouldn't stop to go back and check it out. The nightjar hung tentatively on the dark fringe of my list for years. By the time I eventually did see a genuine Owlet Nightjar (and this time I had witnesses) it had already dropped off my list, but if I had kept it there, I would have, with the 'second' sighting, been able to what they call 'sanitise' my list; that is, replace the dodgy old tick with a new, indisputable one.

Interestingly, I never attempted the same thing with another bird I saw from the car around the same time – a Grey Falcon. If they did exist – which they don't, of course, (*see* GREY FALCON) – and my father had stopped the car, I have no doubt that I would have Grey Falcon on my list. It is a bird that I still haven't seen, yet at the time I never even contemplated putting it on my list because of its rarity. I instinctively knew that I could never prove it, and as I am a terrible liar, I must have known that if I couldn't convince myself 100 per cent of the veracity of my sighting, how could I convince others? I guess this is the essential difference between a stringer and a non-stringer (*see* STRINGER).

Where birding differs from golf is that sightings such as my potential Grey Falcon can have ramifications beyond the individual. For if I had claimed such a rare bird as that Grey Falcon, which was a long way out of range, two things could have happened. Firstly, other birders may well have headed off to try and twitch it, which when they failed to find it would have been a minor personal tragedy for them; secondly, and more importantly, that sighting could have gone down on various databases and affected conservation outcomes.

This can be a serious matter. If conservation land managers have been arguing that old-growth forests need to be preserved with corridors linking them because certain species are incapable of crossing areas of unsuitable habitat in order to colonise patches of good habitat, and somebody mistakenly claims that species hundreds of kilometres away, the entire carefully researched conservation case suddenly looks shaky.

This is why verification can be so important, and why birders are so keen to protect their reputation. As one birder put it, 'Reputation, like virginity, can only be lost once.' If you make an outlandish claim that can't be backed up, people will give you the benefit of the doubt maybe once or twice. But if such unverified claims continue to come in, that well-earned reputation can easily fray.

I am lucky, in part because I am probably too conservative in what I claim, but so far every major rarity that I have found by myself others have subsequently been able to verify. This is why, as far as I am aware, nobody has raised any doubts about the integrity of my *Big Twitch* total – not so much because people thought I was a gun birder, but because other people were with me to see all the rare stuff I saw, and every bird that I saw by myself wasn't unusual enough to raise eyebrows. But if I was queried, I feel I could defend myself robustly because I am 100 per cent convinced within myself of everything that I saw. Anything I had the slightest doubt about I did not add to the list. It cost me three extra species, but I felt to add them to the list could have brought the integrity of the whole list crashing down.

 ACTION: With the price of digital cameras coming right down, it really does pay to have one at hand whenever you are out birding. You never know when something crippling might turn up and even just a blurry record shot is better than nothing (*see* CRIPPLER).

Victoria / the most densely settled but also the smallest mainland state; like little brothers and sufferers of small-man syndrome, Victoria has the annoying habit of boasting about its achievements really loudly to show that it belongs in the same league as the big boys.

Which is why, as a Victorian birder, I feel compelled to point out that despite its size Victoria has a vast array of habitats, leading to a state list of around 530 species. Since the Helmeted

Honeyeater was lumped with Yellow-tufted Honeyeater, the state no longer has any endemic species, though the introduced Song Thrush is found nowhere else in Australia. Other specialties that are more easily seen in Victoria include Pilotbird, Red-lored Whistler, Mallee Emu-wren and Rufous Bristlebird, and wintering Orange-bellied and Swift Parrots.

As the state is so compact, many of the best birding areas are relatively easy to get to. Werribee Sewage Farm is one of the great birding experiences of the country, but other equally rewarding areas for the birder include the Hattah-Kulkyne National Park, Terrick Terrick National Park, the Bendigo region, Chiltern and Mallacoota. There are many more places in between that serve up a fantastic array of birds. The pelagics of Port Fairy, and occasionally Portland, are some of the best in the country, although due to the treacherous nature of the Southern Ocean almost one in two boat trips are cancelled.

There are more birders in Victoria than any other state. And typical of Melburnians trying to prove to the world that they are as important as Sydneysiders, the two national birdwatching organisations – Birds Australia and Bird Observation annd Conservation Australia – are based in Melbourne (*see* BOCA, BIRDS AUSTRALIA).

Visiting birders / people coming into a region from elsewhere for birdwatching purposes; the type who will show little interest in the local cathedral or art gallery, but get very excited at the mention of the local sewage farm.

Often birders to a new region will make mistakes that a local would never make. Sometime it comes about because a visiting birder arrives in an area armed with a list of birds that are supposed to occur there, and what do you know, manages to see them easily. Often this is because they haven't actually put as much effort into identifying the bird as they would if they were birding closer to their home turf. There seems to be less fear of being labelled a stringer (*see* STRINGER) the further away from home you are – just as people on holiday are far more likely to indulge in risky behaviours such as getting drunk and having a casual fling. Because you are away from your comfort zone, and most importantly away from those who know and can judge you, your standards tend to slip a little.

A classic example of this is with Zitting Cisticola around Darwin (*see* ZITTING CISTICOLA). Traditionally, about the most accessible site for them in Australia, at least in terms of easy access, is Holmes Jungle Swamp on the outskirts of the city. Practically every birder who goes to Darwin visits Holmes Jungle, and most of those walk away happily with the bird ticked on their list.

But have they really seen Zitting Cisticola?

What many don't realise (or conveniently choose to ignore), is that Zitting is not the only cisticola at the swamp. The Golden-headed Cisticola, which also occurs in swampy ground near the coast throughout Australia, is also present. In breeding plumage, the male Golden-headed does indeed have a distinctive golden head that the Zitting does not. But the females don't have the bright head, and for much of the year neither do the males. The two species can usually only be separated with much difficulty and then on very close scrutiny.

In breeding season, the Zitting Cisticola is admittedly very conspicuous and performs obvious display flights giving its characteristic call. For the rest of the year it is incredibly cryptic and nowhere near as easily seen as the Golden-headed. But as soon as a visitor birder spies a cisticola lurking out in the grassland, it will inevitably be ticked as a Zitting.

The same phenomenon can happen at the other end of the spectrum where a visiting birder will get a glimpse of what they think is a common bird that they are familiar with at home, and put it down on their list without a second thought. But what they don't realise is that this particular bird may be very unusual in the district. There are many reports from the Broome area of White-bellied Cuckoo-shrikes. Probably 100 per cent of them come from out-of-towners just passing through. None of the local birders I have spoken to has ever seen a White-bellied Cuckoo-shrike; they only see Black-faced Cuckoo-shrikes in Broome. The two can be easily confused, so it is not a hangable offence, but many of these records make their way onto databases and so it appears that White-bellied Cuckoo-shrikes do occur in Broome. It's self-perpetuating: when queried, the visiting observer points to the previous records to justify their call, and so the cycle continues.

Of course, it can work the other way, and sometimes visiting birders are the ones to find the new discoveries. It is as if they are looking at the countryside and its birds with fresh eyes. Even in areas where somebody goes birding almost every day, it is amazing how the really good stuff gets seen first by an interloper. I know of one Melbourne birder who, three decades ago, moved to Brisbane and told astonished locals that he had been seeing Large-billed Scrubwren in the rainforest on the outskirts of Brisbane. The conventional wisdom among this set of birders was that the Large-billed was a bird of higher elevations and hence they had never bothered to look hard enough at the local scrubwrens.

 ACTION: Before visiting a new area, it is always advisable to do a little research on what you are likely to see.

Wader / around 78 members of this extensive family of waterbirds have been reliably sighted in Australia; includes such birds as snipe, plovers, sandpipers, curlews and stints. Also known as shorebirds in American terminology, which is now finding favour here, especially in conservation circles. I have to admit I now use it frequently, as saying 'wader' somehow makes me feel like a backwater yokel.

The waders are the real deal when it comes to birdwatching and twitching. Around 53 of the species recorded migrate here from the Northern Hemisphere, some of which are vagrants (*see* VAGRANTS). On their breeding grounds, many species of wader are dressed in their finest, most colourful breeding plumage, while in Australia they are almost all decked out in muted, drab greys and browns. Many of the species look very similar and can be incredibly difficult to tell apart, especially when there are a whole bunch of North American counterparts to throw into the mix. (Most of our birds come from Siberia, Japan or China.)

It's little wonder then that many birders throw their hands up in bafflement and won't go near waders because they are too hard to identify and these people have better things to do in life than study the tertial projection on small grey bird 15 centimetres long from a distance of 150 metres (*see* TERTIALS). But this is exactly the sort of challenge that sets the heart of a wader afficionado ablaze. If you want to strut your stuff in the birding world, the wader scene is the place to do it.

And what an attractive world it is. If the birders you know are pedantic, suspicious, competitive and secretive, then magnify that 50 times for the wader buff. As a bonus, they get to spend a lot of long summer days exposed to the heat in beautiful and fragrant places such as sewage farms, saltworks and tidal mudflats.

But still, I must admit to yielding to the waders' attractions at times, partly for the challenge, partly because, being highly mobile, they are the group of birds most likely to turn up a new sighting, but mainly because they are remarkable little critters. These little guys (a Red-necked Stint weighs only 25 grams – that's the amount of fat content in a Big Mac) manage each year to fly all the way down from the Arctic Circle to get here, sometimes doing stretches of up to 3000 kilometres in one hop.

Waders lead an extraordinary life, and I feel we should be doing all we can to make their stay a fruitful one. On the East Asian flyway that they choose to migrate along, waders are still caught for food, and much of their coastal estuary habitat is being drained and reclaimed for agriculture and industry. Here in Australia they have it a lot better, but we have no room for complacency. We too continue to drain our wetlands, and those that remain, particularly in coastal areas, are being encroached upon by 'sea change' urban development. All these birds want to do while they are here is to feed like fury in order to build up their fat reserves so that they have the strength to return to their far-off breeding grounds.

Being birds that feed in the open, they can't just duck into the nearest bush when danger approaches. Their only defence is to fly off from potential threats in large flocks – safety in numbers. This means that every time one of us walks dogs through a wetland feeding ground, or rides our bike or otherwise intrudes into their habitat, they are very likely to take to the wing, wasting precious energy reserves. At the very least they will stop feeding to wait for the all-clear, and that's precious feeding time wasted.

 ACTION: When in wader habitat (an estuary, wetland or mudflat), be conscious of whether there are birds feeding and try and alter your activities so as to not disturb them. It is also important to alert other beach or wetland users who will have no idea of the impact they are having. Don't be surprised if you cop a bit of abuse, and a 'Gee, it's as if the bloody birds own the beach,' but at least it raises awareness, and most people tend to move the 50 metres or so that makes the difference between a stint or a sandpiper having its lunch or going hungry.

Wader banding / the capture, tagging and release of waders (shorebirds) so that their migratory movements can be tracked.

Every so often a vocal fringe in the birding community will launch an Internet attack on wader banding, saying that it is cruel and the process kills too many birds to justify the scientific benefits. They rarely have any concrete evidence for this claim, apart from a few anecdotal observations of limping birds that also happen to have been tagged while hobbling along the shoreline – as opposed to the dozens of other hobbling birds that haven't been tagged.

Inevitably someone from the wader banding community (an extremely dedicated but seriously obsessive bunch) bites back and a flurry of accusations flies from both sides of the moral high ground. I suspect that the majority of birders side with the wader banders but ultimately the debate drives everyone else to distraction.

Weddings / (*see* COUPLES, GIRLFRIENDS); also known as The Big Hitch.

Amazing as it may seem, many birdwatchers do get married; even twitchers do (*see* GIRLFRIENDS). These days many weddings are held outdoors, so if a twitcher is getting married there is a chance it may be convened in a bush setting, though I haven't heard of anyone getting hitched at a sewage farm . . . yet. If you really want to test the strength of the marriage right from the very beginning, post a mega-rarity on the local birdline the morning of the wedding. A twitcher might forsake all other humans for his bride but I wonder whether that would extend to a breeding-plumaged Spoon-billed Sandpiper?

I was at a wedding where a birder and researcher specialising in endangered parrots were getting married in the middle of a Mountain Ash forest. Now these forests are quite wet, almost rainforest-like, so you can imagine his surprise when halfway through the vows he heard the calls of a Turquoise Parrot, a threatened bird from the dry, inland woodlands.

None of the guests claimed to have heard it. I suggested to him that he was so overcome with emotion that instead of hearing angels singing, he heard parrots. He wasn't buying it, and to this day thinks I planted a recording of the Turq nearby in order to distract him at the altar. I deny all charges, but it is a brilliant idea.

Here are some good song suggestions for a bird-themed bridal dance:

1. 'I Like Birds', The Eels

2. 'I've Got a Nice Bird', Custard

3. 'Blackbird', The Beatles

4. 'Albatross' (not the Fleetwood Mac instrumental; actual recordings of albatross at the nest)

5. 'The Chicken Dance'

Werribee Sewage Farm / now known as the Western Treatment Plant, situated about 35 kilometres from Melbourne; at almost 11 000 hectares in size – that's twice the surface area of Sydney Harbour – 'the Farm' as it is still known in birding circles, is like Disneyland for birdwatchers.

Sewage farms can be great for birds – these are the only places where we ever put water back into the system, and the farms provide a nutrient-rich soup that abounds in micro-organisms. Such conditions provide a feeding bonanza for our beleaguered waterbirds. Even the most rank concrete-basin type sewage works in the smallest country town can attract wildlife, and from Broome to Bendigo, Townsville to Tuggerah, birders have cottoned on and head to them in droves, pegs firmly attached to noses. (Actually, the smell is quite often far less offensive than you would imagine. In a way I quite like the smell of a sewage farm; it's a positive reinforcement, muscle-memory type thing, because so often that faint waft has been in my nostrils when I've been seeing some really great birds.)

But of all the sewage farms in the land, Werribee is undisputed king, for its size, for its diversity of habitats – from the treatment ponds themselves, to tidal mudflats, saltmarsh, freshwater swamps and grasslands – for its diversity of species (around 270 to date) and sheer abundance of birds. In a drought year, when most other wetlands have dried out, well over 100 000 waterfowl and 16 000 shorebirds congregate there. Werribee in such a year is a truly astonishing sight as massive flocks wheel across the sky, all within spitting (or something that rhymes with spitting) distance of Australia's second-largest city.

Werribee is the one place, aside from specific twitches or pelagics, where you are likely to bump into other birdwatchers out in the field. Birdwatching in Australia has traditionally been a solitary pursuit. Even in the most exciting of birding locales (*see* HOT SPOTS) you can go a whole day without seeing another soul, let alone a birder. Some weekends in summer, when there has been a lot of good stuff about, you might see up to six carloads of birders at Werribee in a single day!

Western Australia / Australia's largest state and a long way away from the rest of the country, so distant is it that it sometimes feels like a different country. In fact, for much of their existence, Western Australians wished they were a different country. The rest of Australia sometimes felt the same way, but for some miraculous reason (probably general apathy) Western Australians continue to grace Australia with their continued presence in the Commonwealth (at least, that's how the Sandgropers see the situation).

Western Australia is big, seriously big, covering the western third of the continent. It is easy to forget how big it actually is. If it was a country it would make the top ten in the world in land area. The vastness of the state is reflected in the diversity of its 550-odd species. In the north there are such tropical species as Gouldian Finch, Yellow-rumped Mannikin, Chestnut-backed Button-quail and Great-billed Heron, while down south some of the specialties include Noisy Scrub-bird, Western Bristlebird, Red-eared Firetail, and Rock Parrot. Of the state's fourteen endemics, twelve are found in the south-west corner.

There are many great birding sites to discover as you travel through the West. A few of the best are Kununurra, Derby (the sewage farm can be particularly good), Broome, the lakes to the south of Perth such as Thomsons and Forrestdale Lakes, Pemberton and Albany, particularly Two Peoples Bay.

As befits the most isolated capital city in the world, the people of Perth and the west in general have always run their own show. In a sense they don't care what the eastern states think, and the only peer review they have cared about is that of those in their own state. Until recently there wasn't a huge amount of cross-Nullarbor liaison and birders in the rest of the country wouldn't hear about what was going on in the West until long after it had happened.

 ACTION: Birds Australia has long had a presence in Western Australia and can be contacted at:

c/o the Secretary
BAWA
167 Perry Lakes Drive,
Floreat WA 6014
www.birdswa.com.au

Winter / from June through to August in Australia, not as quiet a season in birding as one might expect. Breeding does slacken off in the period, but there is a lot of movement going on all around the country.

In the far north it's a relatively quiet time of year. There is no winter as such, only a long dry season, where the weather, though still hot, is rather more bearable. If there has been a good preceding Wet, then the waterholes and billabongs will be full for much of the dry season and life is easy. If the Wet didn't really kick in, the water will dry up fairly quickly and times can get very tough in the remaining wetlands as everything crowds in. This makes it a particularly good time for birding and many people make the trek north, where under benign conditions they have a far better chance of connecting not just with the masses of waterbirds but birds like Hooded Parrot and Gouldian Finch, which are forced to come and drink at the few remaining waterholes.

The hard-core birders, however, tend to forsake the north in winter. All the migrants have moved north of the Equator so there is hardly any chance of a rare vagrant turning up. No, all the mad twitchers spend the winter rugging up in their anoraks and beanies and gazing out to sea, sometimes from the deck of a boat, sometimes (when the weather is too rough to set sail) from a windswept promontory. For this is the season when the Southern Ocean seabirds are swept up on massive cold fronts and come crashing against the southern edge of our continent.

On land there is a surprising amount of activity down south. The high-country breeders have come down from the mountains, spending their time in the foothills and the plains; even birds such as Pink Robins will turn up in suburban parks. This is the time of year when many inland woodland trees burst into flower and, in a good year, when the nectar is flowing, the box-ironbark woodlands are alive with a cacophony of honeyeaters, lorikeets and Swift Parrots, the latter up from Tasmania. Also up on the mainland from Tassie is the Orange-bellied Parrot which has researchers and twitchers alike scouring the coastal saltmarshes, often finding only a handful of birds and wondering where the hell the rest of the population have got to.

Meanwhile inland, if it has been a year of good rains elsewhere, the waters will have reached the swamps, attracting masses of waterbirds to breed and build up the stocks to survive the next drought. The nights get down to freezing but outback days are generally fine and glorious and the travelling birder is in seventh heaven. The only thing dampening his enthusiasm when he rolls out the swag at night at the foot of some far-flung sand dune is the thought that they might not have caught the real killer of Peter Falconio.

Xanthochroism / excessive yellow pigmentation in the plumage of a bird.

Not that common, and to be frank, not really all that exciting to anyone but the saddest of bird-nerds. The main interest associated with xanthochroism is that it saves A to Zs like this having a blank on their 'X' page.

Xanthomyza Phrygia / something that starts with X that is actually interesting, *Xanthomyza Phrygia* is the scientific name for the Regent Honeyeater – sadly, now one of our rarest species.

Once large flocks of this pugnacious, strikingly plumaged bird roamed the box-ironbark country of the south-east. Even as late as the 1950s, hundreds would descend on country towns, like Bendigo, vigorously defending their flowering trees from other nectar feeders.

Due to this nomadic nature, they slipped under the radar of environmentalists until it was possibly too late. Because they were an irruptive species – appearing in a district in vast numbers and then not being seen again for a number of years – nobody really missed them, thinking they were always 'somewhere else'. It wasn't until birding networks became better established in the 1970s that it slowly dawned on birders that people elsewhere else weren't seeing Regents either, a trend confirmed in the first Atlas (*see* ATLAS).

By the time it was realised that the remaining Regents were in trouble it was almost too late to do anything about it. From the gold rush on, their woodland home has been severely depleted, a process that still continues to this day – much of the firewood for our cities comes from remnant box-ironbark forests. In the year before the last drought, only seven Regent Honeyeaters were found in Victoria. In New South Wales the situation is slightly better with over 200 still occasionally gathering during winter and early spring in the Capertee Valley, about three hours drive west of Sydney. Some birds still turn up further north, including a few in Queensland's granite belt, but who knows how the latest drought will have hit these birds. Like many other woodland birds, the Regent Honeyeater has probably not had a truly successful breeding season since the mid-1990s. I certainly know that every time I am lucky enough to find one of these stunning birds my twitcher's joy is tinged with an overwhelming melancholy as I realise that this may be the last time I ever see one.

I plan to make the pilgrimage to the box-ironbark again, but I can't help but wonder, given the combination of the latest drought and bushfires (probably made all the more severe by climate change), whether 14 July 2005 will be the last day I will ever have Regent Honeyeater as an entry in one of my daily bird diaries.

ACTION: Get involved in efforts to bring back the Regent Honeyeater through surveying, tree planting, even admin. Much of the work is coordinated by the Regent Honeyeater Recovery Team and the Threatened Bird Network.

On another, practical level, if you have an open fire, try to source your firewood from scrap or plantation timber. Most commercial firewood for sale in the cities comes from either box-ironbark or Red Gum forests which are both very important for a whole swag of woodland species, not just the Regent Honeyeater.

X-chromosome / the sex chromosome that is twice as prevalent in female cells as it is in male cells; very few x-chromosomes are present in the twitching community.

While there are generally more female birdwatchers than male, lady twitchers are few and far between. Of the fifty twitchers that have seen 700 species in Australia (see 700 CLUB) only five are women, a figure which is actually higher than I suspected. There are many possible reasons for this, probably to do with societal and cultural factors, but I suspect that the main reason is that women are simply not as stupidly competitive in the same way that men are.

Year list / where birders keep track of every species they record in a calendar year; possibly my favourite birding game of all.

Keeping a year list makes 1 January in particular a very interesting day; everything you see on that day, no matter how common, is new for that year's list. I have avidly kept a year list since 1980. Without my Asbirders obsession for year lists, I might not have done as much birding as I have (*see* ASBIRDERS SYNDROME). There have been times when I might not have roused myself to go birding, but the impetus for adding birds to the year's total is enough to snap me from my indolence and get me out and reacquainted with some fabulous birds.

My enthusiasm for year lists set me off in 2002 to chase my childhood dream of garnering Australia's biggest ever year list. It wasn't much of a dream, I know, a bit pathetic really, but it was my dream and I ended up achieving it with a record 703 species (*see* THE BIG TWITCH). So there.

Nobody has as yet made a concerted effort to break my record, which suggests that it's either such an awesome figure that it is too daunting to tackle, or that nobody has quite as sad a preoccupation with year lists as I have. I suspect the latter.

ACTION: Even if you are reading this book in October, start a year list now. I am sure you'll be able to remember most of what you've seen with some help from your notebooks and diaries to jog your memory. Once you have one year completed, start again and see if you can beat it. Just make sure you stop when you get to 702, OK?

Young birders / a relatively rare species.

Hanging around with some birders at a coastal wetland one day, waiting for the tide to turn to bring in the waders that were feeding out on the bay (*see* WADER), the conversation turned to who made the best birdwatchers. One person put forward the theory that the absolute guns were all people who had started their interest in birds as kids. Nobody disagreed with this theory though it was a little self-serving as all three of us had just related stories of how we got into birdwatching as children.

Some see birdwatching as like cracking a code, but for me it is like learning a language. Once you have learnt to read you can never look at a series of letters again without arranging them into words. It's the same with birds. Once you have learnt the language, though you may get rusty and out of practice you will always have some idea, some frame of reference every time you see a bird.

Children with their sponge-like capacity to soak up new information, are more likely to get their head around a new language, learning it both more rapidly and more innately than an already-set-in-their-ways adult. Most children have an inherent fascination with the world around them, birds included. Maintaining that fascination throughout the high school years is the challenge. At fourteen you may as well grease down your hair, start wearing a pair of milk-bottle glasses and hang a sign around your neck saying, 'I am a Poindexter, hit me!' as admit you are a birdwatcher.

Thanks to a brilliantly dedicated teacher at my primary school, there was a whole gang of kids who were into birdwatching; and we still managed to be fairly popular with our classmates. By the end of high school I was the only one still at it. I put this down to the fact that around the time the others dropped off birdwatching, I hooked up with some of Australia's best twitchers. All far older than me (the next closest to my age was already driving a car) they included me in their adult world, which for a thirteen- or fourteen-year-old was something in itself. But the real reason I stayed with birding was that twitching had an edge to it. It was an adventure, and the idea of dashing off on all-night road trips across the state and beyond was one of the coolest things I could imagine.

Unfortunately, in these litigious, fearful, paranoid times we live in, kids like me might not have the same opportunities to get involved with adult birdwatchers unless it is through their parents. Imagine the questions that would be asked these days if a grown man offered to drive a child on a two-day round trip to an outback New South Wales town that nobody has even heard of, where they would have dinner en route in a pub full of bikies and sleep in the car by the side of the road, all in the search of a 'rare bird'? I can see the hosts of the tabloid current affairs shows practising their most condemning scowls already.

 ACTION: Local birding organisations and field naturalist clubs may have juniors sections. One such group is BOCA's Stickybeaks Club, though this seems to be aimed at the pre-teen side of things. For more details check out their website: **www.birdobservers.org.au**

Zitting Cisticola / by far the rarer of the two cisticolas (small marsh loving warbler-type birds), in Australia, the Zitting Cisticola is extremely hard to see (*see* VISITING BIRDERS) and apparently even harder to pronounce.

Nothing gives a beginner away more quickly than mispronouncing the names of birds. It shouldn't matter, but it does, and when I hear an experienced old-timer pronounce 'plover' so that it rhymes with 'clover' (it should rhyme with 'lover'), I can't help but give a misplaced smirk of superiority.

So for the record, if you want to avoid the sniggers of other birders, cisticola should be pronounced 'sis-tick-er-la' with the last syllables running together so that it sounds as though you are saying you have tickled your sister, not as if it was the latest flavour of Coke. And certainly try and avoid, as one friend used to say, 'cisticular'. Particularly with the Zitting before it; people will think you are suffering from a medical condition. 'Sean was a healthy young man until he went to Darwin and picked up Zitting Cisticulars. Now it hurts when he pees.'

So the final bit of wisdom I can impart to you is the following list of the accepted pronunciation of bird names, to help you avoid looking like a duffer when out in the field.

Chough: Looking at the word you might think it would rhyme with cough or plough or even slow, but it is in fact pronounced 'chuff'.

Gerygone: Not Jerry gone (or Gerry with a hard g), but more like Ja-rig-eny, rhyming with aborigine.

Goshawk: Although it is always a delightful surprise to see one, there is no gosh in goshawk. It may sound a little bit naff, but it is actually goss-hawk.

Grebe: For some reason people want to call these waterbirds, grebbies, but grebe is a one-syllable word rhyming with dweeb.

Jaeger: Many people, including the Newcastle netball team named after this seabird, pronounce jaeger with a j, but as it is of Scandinavian origin, it should be pronounced with a y. As in yay-ger.

Pectoral Sandpiper: For years I called this American rarity a Pectorial Sandpiper. There is no 'i'; it should not sound like pictorial. I wish someone had told me earlier as I would have made a total fool of myself for the first six or seven 'Pectorial' Sandpipers I saw.

Prion: Rhymes with iron, not neon.

Curlew: You wouldn't think there was much chance of getting this one wrong. Cur and loo. Curlew. Pretty simple. Yet I knew one young bloke that would get so excited every time he saw an Eastern Curlew that no matter how much he had been coached he would still blurt out 'Eastern Curdle!'

In the end, it doesn't really matter whether he called it a curlew or a curdle. We all knew what he meant, even if it wasn't correct, and who would really deny the passion that the guy obviously had for birds? For when it comes down to it, it is this passion that sparks every birder. The individual may go on to become fascinated by certain aspects of the game – different species, the listing side of it, the numbers, or the science, but every single birdwatcher keeps at it because of that abiding passion. Sure, at times this may lead to some ridiculous behaviour, as the pages of this book have amply demonstrated, but long may it be so, for it makes this pastime all the more glorious.

So I say to every reader: I hope this book has amused and informed but, most of all, inspired you to get out there and find your own curdle!

Acknowledgements

While I take full responsibility for all opinions and alleged facts in this book (I was relying on Big Twitch Institute research after all!), I would like to thank the following people who were happy to help out when I came to them with sometimes the most ridiculous of questions. And sometimes they even managed to have sensible answers. My gratitude goes out to: Adrian Boyle, Alan Morris, Andrew Isles, Andrew Silcocks, Andrew Stafford, Annette Cook, Anthony Watt, Bill Wakefield, Chris Tzaros, David Harper, Dean Ingwersen, Danny Rogers, Graeme Hamilton, Mike Carter, Mike Schultz, Mike Weston, Paul Peake, Peter Lansley, Rob Kernot, Rohan Clarke, Ron Stannard, Ren Millsom, Richard Thomas, Sarah Thomas, Stephen Moss, Suzanne Stannard as well as Russell Woodford and the many contributors to his Birding-aus website whose postings informed, stimulated and occasionally infuriated me as I wrote and researched this book.

I would especially like to thank Paul Peake, who had a look over the first draft of this book and kindly pointed out the bits where I was talking through my cloaca; and also my publisher, Andrea McNamara, who was prepared to go down the horror road of publishing a book about birdwatching for a second time. You'd have thought she'd have learned the first time.

Thanks to Pauline Haas (who has the right obsessive personality to be a gun birder) for her attention to detail in the text design and layout of the book. And to Matt Clare (who wouldn't rate more than a 2 in the quiz on page 11 but who seems to understand birdwatching culture) for cover design and illustrations.

I would also like to acknowledge the Readings Glenfern Fellowship. This provided physical support in the form of a space to write for a year in the wonderful National Trust Victoria building, Glenfern, run by the Victorian Writers' Centre, and moral support simply by showing faith in the slightly odd ideas of one Melbourne twitcher and author.

And, finally, I can't thank my beautiful wife Eleanor enough. She was still willing to marry me despite the bare-faced evidence before her that I was both a writer and a birdwatcher.